BUILDING BUSINESS

BEYOND THE

magnolia
box

BUILDING BUSINESS
BEYOND THE
magnolia
box

Inspiration for entrepreneurs living

in a modern military world

JESSICA SANDS

THIS BOOK BELONGS TO

I am building my dream business that
complements my military life.
A business that gives me the freedom
*to create the life **I truly deserve!***

*I **can** do this & I **will** do this –*
just watch me go!'

CONTENTS

A DEDICATION

This book is dedicated to every military partner who ever felt lost, but found their way anyway.

It's dedicated to those who endured the tours, the deployments, the operations from the home front and still kept smiling.

It's dedicated to those who ever looked at a pile of moving boxes, took a deep breath and just kept going.

It's dedicated to those who have said goodbye to friends, family and their careers and still carried on.

Those who never got asked 'so what is it that you do?' but embraced the conversation anyway.

To every single one of you who took that exciting step into entrepreneurship and to those who are about to do the same.

We are military spouses, partners and other-halves.
The backbone of the UK Armed Forces.
Their greatest cheerleaders and their biggest supporters,
and we can do anything!

This book is especially dedicated to my wonderful Milspos!

It's for you, the ones who have kept going despite all of the challenges. Who stuck it out, embraced it all and kept up. Those who lead the charge and continue to find the path so that others can follow.

It's for you lovely lot who have inspired me in so many ways to become everything that I am today. Thank you for all that you do and for supporting and building one of the best communities I know. We are a movement; we have a voice and we are making a difference.

This book is also dedicated to my wonderful husband. Thank you for being the biggest supporter of military spouses in business and always believing in how important this is to me, even when I stumbled. For all of the times you helped me with this book. For putting up with the tears, the concerns, the worry and, of course, for never letting me give up. Thank you for your constant support both here and wherever you were deployed – for finding that tiny bit of internet in the deepest, darkest parts of the world so that you could check in and support from afar.

Thank you for affording me the opportunities that military life has given us. I am so proud of everything you do in your service with the Royal Air Force (yes, even the crappy bits). You and your colleagues have sacrificed so much for the peace we have the ability to enjoy today and I truly value that. But mostly, thank you for all the tea!

And, I also want to dedicate this book to my perfect son, Elliot. I hope that one day you will read this book with pride, confident with the knowledge that your mum is so much more than just a 'military wife', that we are so much more than a 'dependant' – and that you also get to experience the recognition we deserve.

"If you think the UK Armed Forces are impressive, well you should see what their partners can achieve!"

JESSICA SANDS

Founder of Milspo Network CIC,
graphic designer, podcast host,
business branding expert and author

1

ABOUT THIS BOOK

This book Is written firsthand using snippets from partner testimonials, interviews, podcast episodes and my own experiences of running a business whilst being the wife of an annoyingly busy RAF officer. Its aim is to show you what can be done despite the challenges that modern military life throws at us and I hope it inspires you to follow your own path to create your business.

Throughout this book, you'll find spaces to fill in your own ideas, plans and thoughts about both your military life and business. I encourage you to grab a pen (or pencil... whichever is nearest to you right now) and make this book your own. Scribble on the pages, highlight the paragraphs that speak to you and enjoy every exercise you find along the way.

I've also included a glossary at the back of this book explaining any military terms I've used within these chapters. You might be a seasoned Milspo or new to the gang but, either way, hopefully it will help you to navigate some of the somewhat unusual military lingo that you may not have come across before.

Think of this book as your guide to building the business you deserve. One that will survive postings, deployments and any last-minute surprises you may experience whilst living as a military partner or spouse.

This book is not a complete view on the day-to-day running of a business. Just think, if I were to sit down and tell you in detail about how to use Facebook Ads, how to start an email list or even how to register with HMRC, the information would be out of date far too quickly, you'd be reading forever and you also wouldn't get anything from it. Instead, the aim of this book – as with the original purpose of *The InDependent Spouse* podcast – is to inspire and show you just what you can achieve.

By adding your ideas and sharing them with others in the community, you are helping evolve the conversation around the difference a business can make to our military lives. So, when you're ready,* do come over to the closed Facebook group and share your ideas, your *Eureka!* moments and the exciting plans you have made for your business. I'd love to learn even more about this journey from your own experiences.

So, dear reader, enjoy this book, make it your own and build that business you deserve. I can't wait to see what you achieve and I'll be cheering you on every step of the way!

As I'm sure you're going to get completely stuck into this book once you get started!

2

WHY MILITARY PARTNERS?

"I am: Two of the most powerful words,
for what you put after them shapes your reality."
— Bevan Lee. Australian TV executive and writer

Hello, you lovely lot,

Oh. My. Goodness! It's so amazing to have you here reading my book – did I ever tell you what great taste you have? But in all honesty, thank you so much for trusting in me to help your business and military journey.

Before we get stuck into the business planning side of things, I'm going to use the next few chapters to explain a few things that will help you get the most out of this book.

I'll be introducing myself properly in the next chapter but, before I do, I want to tell you why this book focuses specifically on military spouses and partners.

WHY WRITE A BOOK THAT FOCUSES ONLY ON MILITARY PARTNERS?

As you probably know, we military spouses, partners and other

-halves* find ourselves in a unique situation. Society defines us as one community based solely on the fact that our partners serve in the military. And, because of this, we are the only community I can think of with nothing in common with each other. Yet here we are, thrust together, lumped into one sub-category called *the military partner*.

I often think how strange that is when you consider how very few similarities we have with each other. In fact, if you really think about the one thing that defines our community – our partners' jobs – even those aren't very similar!

In the postings I've had with my husband, I've found myself living next door to commandos, submariners, infantry, engineers, pilots, intelligence officers, divers... all of whom, despite wearing a vast collection of slightly similar uniforms, could not be more varied in their views and needs. So I always find it striking that anyone would think that the partners of this diverse bunch of people should have any similarities either.

As Sarah Stone, founder of the Military Coworking Network, mentioned in her podcast interview with me, *"The one thing we all have in common is that we fell in love with someone whose job is being in the military."*

Which begs the question: *why* would I write a book focused on supporting military spouses and partners in business if we are all so different? If they have nothing in common, how could I possibly help them?

The answer is that even with these fascinating and wonderful differences, fundamentally, military life is tough to experience firsthand. There is an underlying theme from most of the military spouses I have spoken to that, at some point, military life gets a little bit tough. It's likely that if you are a military partner, you'll have felt these tough times too. The result is that a whole load of potential within this community gets lost in the noise and struggles of just being a Milspo. And that's the last thing that this underrepresented community needs.

What I have also seen from my years spent in this community and as I interview my guests for the podcast, is that despite this adversity, amazing things can happen – especially if the right support is applied at the right time. People who once found themselves feeling completely lost can transform into the best versions of themselves.

That is why I want to encourage every single member of our community to do exactly that and become the best version that they can be!

"Security is mostly a superstition.
Life is either a daring adventure or nothing."
– Helen Keller. American author, disability rights advocate,
political activist and lecturer

WHAT DOES THE TERM 'MILSPO' MEAN?
Throughout this book, I will be referring to all military partners as **Milspos.**

Milspo quite literally stands for military spouses, partners and other-halves. I came up with it one night when I realised that although most of the public refer to us as *military wives* (thanks, Gareth Malone!), we don't all fall into that category. So, I wanted to give us a more inclusive and all-encompassing name.

MIL(itary) **S**(pouses) **P**(artners +) **O**(ther-halves) = **MILSPO**

This means wives, husbands, girlfriends, boyfriends, partners, widows…
or whatever you choose to identify as - Milspo is entirely inclusive. So, if
you have felt the tough times of military life and still want to start your
own business, this book is for you.

There are many case studies in this book based on what some people
may call the *traditional* military relationship, in which the serving
partner is male, and the non-serving partner is female. However,
I have also included case studies that reflect a more modern, up-
to-date military community that covers all sorts of relationships and
family units, which I find very exciting!

Plus, *Milspo* is WAY speedier for me to write (and for you to read)
each time. Should you still feel like you don't quite fit into the Milspo
acronym, do not fear – you are very much included and this book is
still for you.

WHY INCLUSIVITY MATTERS IN THIS COMMUNITY

Traditionally, Milspos have been referred to as *military wives* and, on
a few occasions, only *Army wives*.

This has always baffled me. It's thought that the term *Army* sums up
the complete Armed Forces. Just listen to any news broadcast about
military operations. They rarely use the word troops or Armed Forces
personnel; it's merely *soldier* or *the Army* – very odd indeed! It's great
if your partner is actually in the Army but a bit rubbish if they aren't. It
means that many of us have felt a little bit left out from time to time.

The thing is, it's not because we RAF and Navy partners are being
oversensitive. It's because we are proud of our partners and want the
world to know just how epic they are – just like you do if your partner
is in the Army. But, when you leave out one part of a community (or in
this case, two big chunks of the Armed Forces), they feel like they no
longer have a place. This is the same for their partners, too.

Imagine if all military partners were simply referred to as *Army wives* – you miss out on a whole chunk of our community.

It can be the same with business networks. Some are established purely for women and others have been created just for mums. Not only is this a little bit mean on the boys and very cruel to those who can't have children, but it's also closing off a whole section of varied opinions and voices that could help your community or network. Plus, it's limiting your exposure to some fantastic business owners and, ultimately, limiting the potential that your business could wield. That's why I am so keen that this book is not only inclusive to all military partners but it's why I'll be encouraging you to do the same with your business networking.

And so, as the modern military evolves and as the world begins to change for the better, it's more important than ever that everyone is included in this community. Military partners are unique and amazing in their own, individual ways, and no one should be left out – that is why Milspo is so inclusive.

Which is all very well and good but *why* do we even have to be labelled at all? I don't want just to be a military partner or a Milspo – I have my own thing going on.

Wait! I know what you must be thinking… It does seem a bit absurd for anyone to define themselves by the occupation of their partner – I can only think of those married to heads of state who might fall into this: US First Ladies perhaps, and maybe the odd footballer's wife. Genuinely, I can't think of anyone else this side of the 1950s who would choose to do that.

But – and I hate to be the one to break this to you – we don't really get to choose when we get popped into this stereotype. Society has decided that we are *military wives* or *military spouses,* and sometimes even *military husbands* depending on who you speak to. Society has dictated that we have this label... Yep, even if we don't want it. They already have an idea as to what we are and how we act.

I suppose you might have the option to just not tell anyone what your partner does for a living, but have you tried it? It's exhausting! Because after all, we live in a world that revolves around the military. No matter where we live or how we work, and despite our best efforts to keep some normality, our lives at some point will be massively affected by our partner's choice of profession more than any industry I can think of.

So, society decides to label us. That isn't a problem. But this is...

WHEN LABELS CAUSE DAMAGE

Here's a tweet from summer 2020 that sums up the reason why the label *military wife* can be so damaging.

Aug 16, 2020

I hate this pandemic. If I wanted to waste my early 20s I would've become a military wife.

Now, I am not going to lie, I was a little bit shocked when I first read this! During a pandemic, wasting your time is the least of your worries but, more importantly, people believe this *military wife* stereotype to be true!

People genuinely believe that military wives, husbands, spouses, partners – Milspos – waste their days following the flag and are invisible behind the camouflage.

I *know* that this could not be further from the truth. So why do people still believe it? Why does society still believe it? Why have they been allowed to think it for such a long time? Because, dear Milspo, I am sad to say that the biggest culprit, the people who have let them believe this nonsense, is the military partner community itself!

WHY IT'S OKAY TO BE DEFINED BY YOUR PARTNER'S JOB AND HOW WE ARE GOING TO MAKE IT AWESOME!

I used to fight against the label of military spouse. I have hidden it in job interviews, lied about it to new friends and avoided bringing it up in conversation. I was embarrassed and that embarrassment led me to hide from that label. But, by doing that, I was handing control over to others. I was giving away one of the few chances I had to define myself and redefine a stereotype.

I don't want that. I now find myself in a fantastic community that I am proud to be a member of. I want to claim that term and define it my way – with the true definition. I am proud of being a military spouse, not embarrassed by it. Because after all, if I don't own the label and fight against the stereotypes that other people are allowed to make, that stereotype will never change. They will always be allowed to write the narrative and assume that what they have seen before is fact. I want to show the world that you can be a business leader, an entrepreneur, a fantastic parent or none of those things as *well* as being a military spouse, not *despite* it. The two options aren't mutually exclusive.

So, if I go into those job interviews and those conversations, and I own the label of military spouse and show people a different truth – the REAL truth – then, actually, things *can* change.

By changing the conversation around military spouses, it paves the way for those that follow.

For example, I used to work in children's publishing. During our first posting, I spent three months working as a designer, covering maternity leave in a very prestigious publishing house. I'd already applied for a full-time role in the same company but, because they knew I was a military wife, they didn't offer me the job. They even said in the interview that they couldn't employ me because I would be moving in a few years, but they were happy to take me on for the maternity cover.

By the end of the three months' cover, they were (frustratingly) right; it was time for me to move on – we were posted. However, and here's the important part, during those three months, their opinion towards military spouses and how they worked did a complete U-turn. I like to think that the next time they encountered a military spouse, they would change their unconscious bias and employ them.

Which is why I encourage you to grab hold of your Milspo title and embrace it – show the world just how amazing you are because it doesn't just help you, it helps us all.

> *"The secret of change is to focus all your energy,*
> *not on fighting the old, but on building the new."*
> *– Socrates. Father of Western philosophy*

So let's not be ashamed or embarrassed by our military partner tag. Just because the rest of society buys into a stereotype that isn't true, doesn't mean that we have to buy into it, too. And what's even better? We can shape it and change it!

SO WE'VE GOT THIS LABEL, HOW ABOUT WE CLAIM IT BACK FOR OURSELVES?

We don't have to be what society is telling us to be. We can change the conversation. In fact, I think we have a responsibility to do just that. It's time to own your label as a military spouse, partner and other-half. Embrace it! Show the world how amazing we are because you never know, one day you might end up being the next Milspo applying for that job, right after someone has paved the way. It's going to make your life a damn lot easier if that employer knows precisely how epic we are (and it also stops that nonsense on Twitter!).

This book is to help you do exactly that! To support you in becoming amazing Milspo business owners – ones who break stereotypes and shake up what society thinks.

Now that's sorted, let's talk about the real difference this community can make for each other.

YOU CANNOT BE WHAT YOU CANNOT SEE

"The fastest way to change yourself is to hang out with people who are already the way you want to be."

– Reid Hoffman. LinkedIn co-founder

I think it's crucial that, as Milspos, we have access to people from our community who have achieved something great. People who can inspire us and, most importantly, share with us how they got there.

We know that military life can be challenging and confusing. For a long time, we have not been able to see those fantastic people in our community. They've been hiding behind their serving partner. And that makes it fiddly if you're living in this world looking for like-minded people to inspire you.

But, happily, times are changing and these inspirational people are finally getting their voices heard.

Within this book's pages, I feature many Milspos I have met over the last 12 years of my military life. I hope that when you find them, you get excited by their stories and go on to find out more about them. They are indeed an epic collection of people. Many I now consider genuine friends. Like all military friends, they are scattered far and wide but have a vast experience of the military world from all angles of Armed Forces life. They are business owners, veterans, award winners and game changers. I am so excited to share their stories with you in the hope that they help impress, inspire and make your life that little bit better.

So, dear reader, grab your favourite pen (you'll need one) and let's start building the business of your dreams!

I like to call us Milspos – I'll explain why later.

3

WHO ARE YOU, JESS?!

We've probably already met at some point over in the Milspo community or maybe you found me through *The InDependent Spouse* podcast series. Either way, I love that you are here, and I can't wait to share with you everything I have learnt along the way. But first, you should probably know why and how I got around to writing this book, and why I think it's okay for you to take business advice from me.

> *"Character cannot be developed in ease and quiet.*
> *Only through experience of trial and suffering can the soul be*
> *strengthened, ambition inspired, and success achieved."*
>
> *– Helen Keller. American author, disability rights advocate,*
> *political activist and lecturer*

I believe you really can't be an expert, especially not a business expert, without running your own business first! That is why everything

I share in this book is taken from my own experience of running my business from my military married quarter through countless moves, deployments and the challenges that come with military life. I also believe you can't know it all and you should always be learning, which is why, at the parts of this book that I don't know the answers to, I'll be calling on my business best pals to help.

Now, I am not one to bang on about how experienced I am, but I think it's important for you to know my background in business as well as with the military community so that you are comfortable with the advice I share with you.

SO, HERE'S MY STORY...

Rewind to 2009: smack bang in the middle of the Afghanistan conflict and about six months after I had fallen in love with an RAF officer. Exciting, hey?! And yet, as you probably know, the reality is a little bit different from what you see in *An Officer and a Gentleman*.

I was enjoying a fantastic career as a graphic designer creating stationery and children's books for Disney. I lived in beautiful Bath, worked in my dream job and had found the man I was planning to marry. Life was great!

And then, that posting notice arrived.

My boyfriend was posted, along with the whole C-130 Hercules fleet from RAF Lyneham (so close to Bath) to RAF Brize Norton in Oxfordshire (not so close to Bath).

He commuted from our home in Bath to Brize Norton for a whole year, adding three hours to his already long day. By the time he'd experienced one miserable snowy winter of dangerous driving on the M4, including three short-notice medevac flights from Germany and Afghanistan, he had had enough. This was when one of us had to choose between our careers and our lives together – a conversation that most military families have had at one time or another. We decided together that my design work could be made more flexible by leaving my job and starting work as a freelancer. It was my career that took the hit so that our relationship wouldn't.

That August, I resigned from my job. A week later, I left Bath and we moved into a private rental near RAF Brize Norton. I had lived in Bath for ten years. It was where I had completed my degree, where I had worked in my career over six years, it was where my friends and family were – what had I done?!

Initially, it went well. I spent my time exploring the local area and networking but, as we moved into winter and my boyfriend's work become even more operational, I spent more and more time alone. You see, that's the thing with RAF bases. They seem to be in the middle of nowhere and with few opportunities, which sucks when you're a 25-year-old with very little to do. You never really realise the importance of company and friends until you don't have them.

Apart from doing the big shop, going to the odd wives coffee mornings on the base and monthly networking groups, I barely spoke to anyone.

I attempted to get a job at two local and very well-known book publishers but, as soon as they'd worked out I was a military wife, I was told that my application was no longer needed. So, I did what I knew I could do and got stuck into building my business, attempting to make it as a successful freelancer…it didn't go well.

I was utterly miserable. I had lost my role in the world and was no longer getting the consistent design work that I had initially, as my clients in Bath began to forget me.

In 2014, we were married and moved into our first married quarter, or service family accommodation (SFA), but nothing changed.

I finally told my husband just how bloody miserable our new life was making me. It was when we were taking a much-needed holiday to Antigua to get to know each other again as a result of too many deployments and one day, after a few too many cocktails, I finally told him how very miserable and lost I was. Together we realised that it was my little design business that made me happy and maybe it was that which could pull me out of the slump.

I had found an online business course that looked promising and I spent all of the money I had made in my business on this last attempt at salvaging something for me. That course was completely life changing. I now had monthly business-building challenges to complete and a whole online network to tap into. It encouraged me to go networking, build my email list and start finding new clients online rather than relying on clients who needed me 'in-house'. Although the first few months were financially challenging, by the summer of 2016 and our new posting to Northwood HQ, I finally had a business and a client base that I could take with me anywhere.

It was in this second posting that I realised I couldn't be the only one who felt this way. I couldn't be the only partner who was lonely and longing to create a new and transient business – I just needed to find them.

Here's a diary entry that I wrote just a few months later....

25th November 2016,

I am considering launching a Milipreneurs project – my members site – a place for female military spouses to get business support but belong to a network.

I think a second business would technically be simple for me to launch. It'll take a lot of research and my time, and I hope it will appeal as I am a military wife but it's frightening, too! I wonder how many military dependants there are in the UK – Milspouses will be the focus of the concept.

And that's precisely what I have done. The Milspo Business Network is a community of the most remarkable military spouses, partners and other-halves creating the most epic businesses despite the pressures of modern military life... but that's also a straightforward thing for me to say now. The reality was quite different.

Once I had worked out that I needed to create my network of people who just got it, I decided to start a networking group with the idea that there could be a networking group in every military base. I'd joined two Military Wives Choirs by now and I loved the fact that I could just slot seamlessly into the new one every time I moved. So, it seemed like a no-brainer to do the same for business owners.

In winter 2016, Milipreneurs was launched on Facebook. There were 30 members in the first week, with our first meeting booked at the base community centre for the following Wednesday. The group was only for wives (I hadn't quite learnt then) and, actually, it was really good fun... even if there were only ever four of us that turned up each month.

The networking turned into a wine club in classic military style and sadly fizzled out, but the dream never left, which is why the second attempt came through the agency Forces Enterprise Network (FEN) Hub.

FEN was started in 2015 by Heledd Kendrick, Nadine Monks, Sarah Walker and Christine Dedman to support small business owners in the military community and I always had a soft spot for it. These four amazing women embodied everything that I believe a military spouse in business stands for. They had drive, focus and were running epic established businesses – they were also raising their families so were incredibly short on time. Sadly, the glorious FEN now exists as a dormant company – it just wasn't the right time. But I learnt so much from the days of FEN and am so grateful to have been a part of it.

Inspired by the many military partners I had met during the Milipreneurs and the FEN days, I wanted to share their stories with a larger audience, which is why *The InDependent Spouse* podcast was born. If you have listened to any of the interviews I have held with these military partners, you'll know just how much I love their stories and how connecting, and networking, helped found the idea for the Milspo community.

It was clear from very early on that everyone loved the podcast series – it's now reached over 17,500 downloads in over 20 countries. Still, I wanted to connect these inspirational people to even more of our community. And I managed to do that through online networking sessions, this time from our third posting at RAF High Wycombe HQ.

My lovely business best friend was continually telling me that her best ideas came to her when she was away from her computer and she was not wrong. Mine came to me in two parts: the first when changing lanes on the M4. By this point, I'd had four houses since I met my husband and, on this occasion, I'd started to drive on autopilot to the last place that I'd lived. It wasn't the first time I had done this and I'm sure it won't be the last, but this time, it really upset me. I had a great networking group at that posting but, as I was only there for a year, I had to leave them when we moved. They'd forgotten me but I missed them.

The second *Eureka!* moment came a few weeks later, whilst paying for *The InDependent Spouse* podcasting software. I had attended an online business party on Zoom, where the host had used breakout rooms – I was trying to work out if I could add breakout rooms to my account and whether it would be possible to use them for networking. Someone in the US was already doing this and they called it *Virtual Networking*. They were having so much success! It seemed to be the perfect solution for the military spouse community.

I found nothing similar in the UK, which sort of makes sense when you think about it. If you wanted to do business networking, you would go to a *real-life* group because that's just how it's done (or at least it used to be).

I had found a perfect solution. Not only could we network together, no matter where we were posted, we could also put all that expertise we have, using online video calls when our partners are away, to good use – it was a win-win!

Now I just had to get my head around the technology – cue one very comedic night of me, my long-suffering husband and my poor sister 'zooming' each other via any mobile phones, laptops and iPads we could find in some multi-screen carnage, just to see if it could work. I can still hear the feedback ringing in my ears but, you know what… it bloody worked.

So, in May 2019, with my poor husband on admin support, we tested the concept with 12 business owners all over the UK (and one in Germany). It was a massive success!

Connections were made, online business ideas were brought to life and, most importantly, Milspo business owners were no longer limited to networking by location. These members were inspired, happy and building connections, even mentioning how it was the first adult conversation they'd had all day. One attendee's husband had recently received an admin order for Germany and, not knowing anyone there, now had a new friend who already lived there just by turning up to that first meeting. It worked!

This idea, which was dreamt up all because I didn't focus properly on the M4, is now helping military spouse business owners all over the UK (and the world) connect and talk about business properly. I love these events. They are encouraging and safe meeting spaces where connections are built, and friends are made.

I am so proud of those early, rickety days of virtual networking and how it kick-started the Milspo community, and I am super proud that they have been tried, tested and evolved into what they are today. They have given me access to a wide range of business owners that I wouldn't usually have met, and it is something that has remained an integral part of the Milspo offering.

Since then, I have been recognised by Small Business Britain as one of the #ialso 100 Top Business Owners in 2018, as an f:Entrepreneur Top UK Female Business Owner, have been asked to make a speech at the House of Lords and am a Prince's Trust mentor, all because of this military life I find myself in.

So now, years later, after the idea having taken many different forms, Milspo encompasses everything that I was missing in that first posting. This community just get it and I love connecting with them as well as introducing them to one another. We have an online community, chances to network, Christmas parties, awards nights and some truly great friendships. I can soak up all the excitement of others in business and find like-minded business leaders just rocking this military life!

Choosing this life was hard. In all honestly, I never actually wanted to run my own business (and I'll go into more of that in the next few chapters) but, after 10 years in the business, I just love it! Honestly, self-employment in this military world is just epic!

I cannot wait to share with you all the good, bad and ugly parts so that you can get to experience it too – shall we get started?

Are you ready to start your own posting-proof business?

"If you don't build your dream, someone will hire you to help build theirs."

- Tony Gaskins.

Motivational speaker, author and life coach

PART ONE

HOW TO DO IT

ARE YOU READY?
HERE'S SOME TIPS TO GET YOU STARTED

I bet you are raring to get going in your business but, the question is, where to start?

I'm sure you've seen many Milspos running their successful businesses and you've dreamed of being there one day, too. The best news? They all started exactly where you are now.

Over the next few chapters, I'll be exploring the reasons why you might be interested in fitting a business around a busy military life and how you can turn this vision into a reality.

Part One is chock-full of activities and exercises for you to complete if you haven't yet started your business but don't skip past them if you've got your business up and running already. You can still get a lot from them and can use the activities and exercises to re-affirm and strengthen your business foundations – you might even get some fresh ideas for your business that may help you grow in ways you hadn't even imagined yet!

In Part One we'll be covering:
- Why becoming an entrepreneur fits military life so well
- The key reasons you'll want to have a business so that you can be inspired every day
- What type of business you're going to run
- Whether there is an actual need for your product or service
- Whether you can make money from it
- If your business is going to get you excited on a daily basis
- Whether it can be transient
- If it's the right time to launch a business
- How to name your business
- How to claim that name so you can use it commercially
- What HMRC expects from you as a business owner
- Whether you'll be running as a sole trader, limited company or something else
- What you'll need to keep accounts for your business
- Who you'll need to ask permission from to start your business
- Why you should be insured

So, what are you waiting for?! Grab a pen and let's start planning your dream business!

4

WHY RUNNING YOUR OWN BUSINESS FITS WITH MODERN MILITARY LIFE

"Every great dream begins with a dreamer.
Always remember, you have within you the strength,
the patience, and the passion to reach for the stars
to change the world."

– Harriet Tubman. American abolitionist and political activist

I've spoken previously about why I started my own business. Now it's your turn to investigate whether starting a posting-proof business might just be what you need to achieve your own dreams whilst living in this military life.

So why, as a Milspo, is it so amazing
to run your own business?

YOU CAN CONTINUE YOUR CAREER...
OR PERHAPS YOU DON'T WANT TO?

Nothing sucks more than leaving a job you love, especially if you're highly trained and love what you do. Unfortunately, that is the reality for lots of us in the military community.

Despite the progression made towards remote working – which was brought even more to the forefront thanks to the pandemic – sadly, when your partner gets that posting notice, you'll most likely need to relocate and you may need to leave your job, too, but that's where self-employment comes in.

One of the joys of entrepreneurship is that you don't have to give up what you love, which means you can continue to build on your previous experience within that sector. Although there are many differences between full-time employment within a company and being self-employed, the latter style of work can be a great way to stay within your industry whilst you move around.

However, you might want to move away from the industry you already work in. So, what better opportunity to try something new?

IT CAN PROVIDE MORE FLEXIBILITY AROUND MILITARY PLANNING... OR LACK THEREOF!

Military life can be all over the place. One day, you might be asked to move to a new house with very little notice or be left as the sole carer for your entire family for up to nine months – sometimes, these happen at the same time! And there aren't many employers who are going to truly understand when this happens. The brilliant part of having your own business is that you get to decide when you work and where from.

Now that I am my own boss, I can organise work to fit into my increasingly hectic life and be flexible enough to deal with any detachments and postings that come our way. I know that when my husband is away on deployment, I can be selfish and commit 110% to my business. However, I also know that if he arrives home early (or, the more inevitable, late), I can shuffle the majority of my work around those dates.

As a service provider, I also know that as long as I have my laptop, a workspace and a bit of Wi-Fi, I can pretty much work anywhere. I have purposely built my business to be transient in the face of military life.

It can be a bit more challenging as a product-based business, especially if you invest in premises. With that said, thanks to the way consumers are buying products online nowadays through platforms such as Amazon and Etsy, you can run very successful businesses virtually. One of the few positives to come out of the pandemic is that it has revolutionised the way in which consumers buy and there are no longer any major concerns about buying online. These shopping platforms are perfect if you need flexibility and, just like my service business, don't rely on a specific location as they can be accessed anywhere with a bit of internet.

A BOOST IN FAMILY INCOME

Leaving your job doesn't just mean you leave something you love; it also means you leave behind the financial security, i.e. the stable salary, that comes with it.

When we were first posted, we quickly discovered that our household had become £30k worse off as a result. That has never sat well with me. I knew my husband couldn't be the only one generating income for our marriage to be balanced. This is one of the key reasons I started my business.

Do you remember that '90s classic, 'The Sunscreen Song'? There's a lyric towards the end of the song that has always stood out to me.

It talks about how you shouldn't expect anyone else to support you financially, whether that's a trust fund or a wealthy spouse, because either could run out.

Having my own income means that I can contribute, as well as giving me some freedom to be independent, too.

YOU CAN EXPERIENCE SOME AMAZING THINGS!

During the time I have been running my own business, I have had some fantastic experiences. Away from the daily admin and the fun I have creating beautiful brands, I have run workshops and presented in some prestigious locations.

Not only that, having a business means I get to network and meet some wonderful people, many of whom I now consider to be great friends. We are all like-minded individuals and incredibly supportive of one another, which is especially important when you find yourself spending so much time away from family and friends.

Sometimes, the combination of running a business alone and living the military life can be quite a lonely affair. Still, I know that the network I have built up, both in my current posting and virtually, means that I will never truly be alone.

IT CAN TRAVEL WITH YOU, ANYWHERE YOU GO

If you're like me and you set out to make your business transient, then, when it's time to pack those boxes and head off to a new quarter, you'll be able to set up and continue what you were doing before at your new location almost seamlessly, without causing too much damage to your business… if any at all! (Don't worry, there's an entire chapter on how to run a business through a military posting later on in the book.)

Changing locations every two to three years is not ideal and there is always a knock-on effect when it comes to your client turnover each time you move. But, as long as you're clear in your communication with your clients and customers that service may not operate as usual during those times and you have some firm foundations and systems in place, self-employment is a great way to work as a military spouse.

IT'S FUN!

I bloody love my business! It's given me freedom, purpose and a real sense of achievement.

Yes, it can be hard work when you're up against a deadline but the results you get from your hard work will always be amazing.

If you're a military spouse thinking of running your own business that can survive active military service life, deployments, tours and postings, then do it! It can be a wonderful thing. As a designer, I've created my own business that allows me the freedom to work from anywhere we're posted to. And I am not the only one either. There are many business owners just like me located all around the country (and beyond) doing the same.

YOUR KEY REASONS FOR BEING IN BUSINESS

There are so many positives surrounding military life and starting your own business but, in order to give yourself the best possible chances of success, it's essential to recognise these early on. These ultimately become the key reasons that will help you keep going 'When the Going Gets Tough' – to quote my favourite Billy Ocean song!

Because the harsh reality is that although running a business is completely epic, there will be some tough days, too, and that's why it's so important to work out what your key reasons are so that you can stay inspired and keep that 'dream in motion'.* Because you don't want anything standing in the way of your dream business and what it can achieve.

TIP: I often keep my key reasons somewhere close to me in my office. That might be a list of reasons or a single image or collage from Google detailing exactly what I am working towards. For example, if I want to contribute to a holiday or win a particular award, I'll keep that key reason close by so that it's front and centre of my attention when I need the pick-me-up to stay motivated during those tough days.

* And yes, it's completely normal that you've still got Billy Ocean's song stuck in your head as, I'm not sure if you could tell but, it was in mine the whole time I spent writing this chapter. You're welcome!

WHY DO YOU WANT TO START YOUR OWN BUSINESS?

In the space below, write some personal reasons as to why you want to start your own business. Focus on what's important to you and visualise how it would feel to achieve those things you want most from life. What difference might it make to you and your family? Have some fun with this one and dream big!

5

THE PRACTICAL SIDE OF STARTING YOUR OWN BUSINESS

"Every problem is a gift—
without problems, we would not grow."

— Tony Robbins. American author, coach, speaker and philanthropist

The previous exercise on page 42 has got to be one of my favourite parts of business building and is probably the most important part when you're getting started, too. I'm so excited that you've finally found your key reasons for running your business that you can keep right beside you from now on. But it's not all about the positives of starting a business. You also need to think about the practicalities of starting your own business.

Next up, you need to decide on some of the details about your business. You might have some of these ideas already mapped out and, if you're an established business, you might already have these written down in your business plan.

Even if you think you are already established in your business, don't skip this part! Reviewing these details from time to time can help you realign your business plans and move you closer to that end goal.

WHAT IS IT THAT YOU'RE GOING TO DO?

You need an idea to start a business. I was lucky; I knew from an early age that I loved to design, so it was easy for me to move into freelancing before launching my agency.

However, it might not be so clear to you. Maybe you're a keen crafter who creates beautiful pieces that your friends have always asked to buy. Or perhaps you have a flair for making birthday cakes for your children and have had a few friends ask you to bake some for theirs. Maybe you were an accountant or assistant in your previous career, and you still have the drive to do this. These are key strengths that can be transformed into something commercial.

ARE YOU ALREADY WORKING FULL-TIME IN A JOB YOU COULD MAKE INTO A BUSINESS?

If you're already working in an industry you love and believe you could create your own business within that field, then you're onto a great start. Many of the businesses I work with started their companies alongside their primary job and grew it from scratch during their evenings and weekends – it's called a side-hustle. Doing it this way means you can build up your client list whilst you still have a monthly income and the stability that comes with employment. This is exactly how I started. I worked full-time in a design agency and then took on extra clients in my free time.

Now, I must admit that this was backbreaking work, and I spent far too many hours designing, but, with enough self-care and motivation, I built up my client list and went completely freelance. But, be warned: if you are in a job where you could have issues with client overlap and conflicts of interest, then be sure to check your contract thoroughly. You don't want to get on the wrong side of your employer, especially if they could become a future client.

ARE YOU ALREADY DOING IT AS A HOBBY?

Think about what you do in your spare time. Perhaps you're into health and fitness and feel that you'd enjoy starting your own running or training business. Maybe you've been into calligraphy for a while and want to monetise it.

If you've already unknowingly started your business as a hobby, then you've probably got enough experience and know-how to move it into a profitable business, especially if you already have the demand from friends asking for your product or service. So, why not get paid for it?

It's time to think about your strengths, what you love doing and whether it could be transferred into something more commercial. What are you good at? What do you enjoy talking about?

Things I *could* do...

Now, narrow the field a bit by thinking about what you actually WANT to do. You certainly might know how to balance an account book, but do you honestly have a love for it?

Things I *want* to do...

And finally, time to get real! When you consider things like available time, location, skill set and work etc., what can you do?

Things I *can* do...

Use the space below to explore these ideas. Focus particularly on the five answers you added in the 'want to do' section. You'll be spending a lot of time running your own business so make sure you love the idea in the first place.

IS THERE A NEED FOR YOUR PRODUCT OR SERVICE?

A lot of start-up businesses fail in their first year for many reasons. One of them might be because people just don't need what you are doing.

Think long and hard about whether there is an existing market for the business you want to create. Research people in the same field who are doing a similar thing and take a look at how they are doing it. If you can't find anyone doing anything similar, the unfortunate reality might be that there is simply no need for it. You might have a fantastic idea for a product but, the likelihood is, if there isn't an audience that is interested in it, then you probably won't be able to turn it into a successful business.

However, if you discover there is an existing industry doing what you do, then you'll undoubtedly have a market.

LET'S DO SOME RESEARCH!

One of the essential parts of a business is the research you do into how appealing you are, so it makes sense to start early – before you even launch your business.

Make a list of companies who are doing something similar to what you are planning to do. They can be huge multinationals or smaller businesses – it doesn't matter.

Company name...
What I like about them...
What they do well...
Where they could improve...

TIP: Try not to be overwhelmed by what others are doing; you'll be able to apply your unique know-how or product to this industry. It's this very knowledge or product that will make you special and what your clients and customers will come back to you for. Remember, you aren't going to copy what they do. You are simply exploring the industry to see if it's a good fit for you.

COULD YOU MAKE MONEY FROM IT?

Running a business can be expensive. You'll probably have overheads and costs you'd need to consider as your business grows, especially if you're a product-based business. However, even if you're a service-based business with low overheads, you'll still need to think about how you're going to make enough income to pay for it.

I hate to say this but, if your business doesn't make a profit, then it's just an expensive hobby and also a bit of a waste of your time. Have a good look at the other businesses doing similar things to see the kinds of prices they're charging for their products and services, as this will help you to work out whether it's still something you can make an income from once you've considered your overheads, production costs and time.

But don't get too disheartened; many businesses struggle to make a serious income within the first few years, and most choose to put any profit they make back into building the business. With hard work and a bit of courage, you can undoubtedly create a company that will not only be transient but can pay you a wage.

LET'S TALK ABOUT MONEY!

Don't worry; working out what you'll be charging isn't as hard as you might think. You need to make sure that if you're working in your business, you are making money from it.

Time to decide... what sort of business are you going to be?

I want you to think of two white T-shirts. One is a £10 tee from H&M and looks a lot like that new Victoria Beckham tee that costs £1,000. They look the same, they're both cotton, both white and both wearable but one costs a hundred times more. Why?!

It all comes down to brand experience.

Taking the above into consideration as well as the research you conducted on your industry, decide what kind of price point you are aiming for and what kind of brand your company will be. You don't need to make any firm pricing decisions now, but it'll help you with the rest of this book's activities.

DOES YOUR IDEA GET YOU EXCITED EVERY DAY?

Running your own business can sometimes be a bit of a lonely existence.

When I am working on a deadline in my studio, I often don't see another human for hours! Even when I choose to work from a co-working space, I still need to get my head down and get my jobs done. It's very different from working in a big company where you see the same people every day – you need to be very self-focused.

What makes all the difference is that I completely love what I do, especially the bits around making business plans and decisions. I get excited every day about working both in my business and on my business. It's so different to working for 'the man'*, and although it's really hard work sometimes, I wouldn't have it any other way. It also means that I can move wherever the MOD posts my husband and, although I miss having office buddies, I get to spend more time with my partner.

There are no two ways about it: you have to be excited about what you chose to do as you'll be doing it every day. So, now is the time to really think about whether you could spend a large chunk of your time doing it.

Imagine you're five years into your business journey: where do you see yourself and your business? Does it still keep you excited? Are you always jumping out of bed in the morning in excitement? Be laser-focused with the fine details of what you are doing. **Use this space to add any ideas that pop up.**

COULD IT BE TRANSIENT?

Here's the best part! Military life means that we could be posted at any time, sometimes every few years. If you build your business to be transient, there should be no reason why you can't continue trading regardless of where you end up living. I've written a whole chapter on this later in the book, which goes into more detail on how you can do it. And believe me when I say, you absolutely can. My little design business has survived six moves since it started, and I have so much to share with you as a result!

I expressly set up my business to be transient so that I could follow my husband with his job. I have great systems in place so that if we had to move next week, all I would need is my Mac and some Wi-Fi – could your business idea do the same?

HOW MIGHT IT FEEL TO HAVE A SUCCESSFUL BUSINESS AFTER A POSTING?

In the space below, write about what it might mean to you and your family to have a business that can move with you when posted.

We aren't going to focus on the negatives here as I have a sneaky suspicion you might already have a couple of excuses as to why you shouldn't get started. Instead, I want you to focus on what a successful transient business might mean to you.

IS IT PRACTICAL TO START YOUR OWN BUSINESS?

Running a business is time-consuming. If you don't think about the exact times in which you're going to work in your business, you'll have clients calling at all hours and making demands of you when you're not available.

However, with proper planning and communication, you can run a business around many of the demands service life has on us. If you have children, you might need to consider childcare (especially if your serving partner is operational) so your business should be making enough money to cover this expense. You might have to think about the location that you might be posted to in the future. If you're expecting a foreign posting, you'll have to look into the legalities of running your business abroad. Or perhaps if you're running a business from your married quarter that relies on clients visiting the house, you'll need to research whether you'll be allowed to have that type of business since the property belongs to someone else.

This may all sound complicated and a little overwhelming, but once you have those plans in place, you'll be prepared for any eventuality.

IS RIGHT NOW THE BEST TIME FOR YOU TO START YOUR BUSINESS?

Okay, let's get sensible. Is it REALLY the right time for you to be launching your business? I know that it's almost impossible to plan within this military world but that doesn't mean you can't get started on making your own plans for when the time comes.

If you have written down reasons as to why right now is not the best time, look at them again and really consider if they are true or whether they might just be excuses because you're a bit hesitant about starting. The second part of this book is all about changing your mindset around business but it's good for you to determine early on any of the barriers you might face along the way.

So, now you should have an excellent idea of...
- What it is you're going to do,
- Whether there is a need for your product or service,
- Whether you can make money from it,
- If your business is going to get you excited every day,
- Whether it will be posting-proof, and
- If it's the right time to launch a business.

Well done, you! That's a good chunk of your business planning complete. By now you should have a good idea of your business and how it will be successful.

You may have also found some sticking points or have questions that can't yet be answered, or you might simply be feeling a little bit miffed at military life. But please don't get disheartened. As long as you've researched, planned and checked through the proper channels, you should be able to keep your business running no matter where you're posted, and there's still a lot more of this book to work through, too.

Running your own business can be very hard work but so rewarding at the same time, especially if you're a military partner who has chosen to follow their serving partner's job. You can do this!

Next up, we are going to dive into your business in even more detail! So, grab yourself a cuppa and some tasty treats, as I'm sure you're going to love this next chapter.

'Working for the Man' – Wow! I've never noticed before how REALLY outdated that phrase is! Maybe one day it'll be 'working for the lady super-boss'. I can't wait!

6

YOUR NEW BUSINESS'S FIRST STEPS AND BUILDING THE FOUNDATIONS

"Don't be afraid of the space between your dreams and reality. If you can dream it, you can make it so."

– Belva Davis. American television and radio journalist

Now that you've worked out why it's a good fit for you to start your business and how well it will fit with your military life, it's time to start thinking about the details. Oh, this is where it gets exciting!

In this chapter, we'll work through what you need to do before you launch.

FIRST THINGS FIRST – LET'S TAKE A MOMENT TO DISCUSS THE DREADED IMPOSTER SYNDROME

At this point in your business start-up journey, you might be feeling a little bit uncertain and out of your comfort zone. You might even feel overwhelmed at points or as if you want to back out. Can you do me one little favour? Just stick with planning until the end of this section on page 105... I promise you, it will all be worth it.

You may have noticed that a tiny negative voice in your head is beginning to tell you lies about how rubbish you are and that your business will never work. Don't you dare listen to it because it's talking complete and utter nonsense. Repeat after me...

> *'This negative voice in my head isn't my truth. I **can** do this and I **will** do this – just watch me go!'*

Feels better, doesn't it? I want you to remember this feeling every time that annoying negative little voice jumps in to ruin your good thoughts. If it helps, every time this happens, replace the voice with the positive saying above and remind yourself that you absolutely can do it.

Ignore that negative voice, embrace all of the new ideas that come to you in this chapter and get them all written down in the activity sections. I promise you can achieve these things even if they feel very out of reach right now.

We'll be covering mindset and imposter syndrome in chapter 10, if you'd like a little boost before you start this part.

And now onto the exciting planning parts!

What's to come is quite possibly the most important bits of planning your business, which go on to make up the essential foundations you need to build your business. You don't particularly need to do these next steps in the order I've written them but you should definitely consider working through all of them at some point before you launch.

TIME TO NAME YOUR NEW ADDITION

You've probably got a fair idea from the last chapter of what your business is going to do and you might have also had some ideas about what you're going to call it, too. But maybe you're struggling or you just have too many options to pick from.

This is so exciting – trust me! Although it might feel daunting now, this part can be really fun. It's time to think of a name for your new business: perfect if you are just starting but also a great little exercise if you aren't so keen on the business name you currently have. You can look at online business name generators but I prefer doing it this way.

Here's a little activity I go through with any of my clients who are struggling to pick a business name.

NAMING YOUR BUSINESS

1. Use the space below to write down any words that you associate with your business. Think about your mission, what you're creating and what your business values are.

2. Next, use a thesaurus to see what associated words you can link to the terms you noted down in the first step and add them below.

3. Time to re-check your competitor list from chapter 5. Doing this will give you a feel of the names currently associated with your industry and provide you with an idea of the current trends. You don't want to stray too far away from the terms that they use because you don't want to confuse your clients and customers. Use the space below to write down the words or phrases that you love and, just as importantly, the ones you hate.

4. Consider new trend start-up names. For example:

- Snappy one-word names, such as Uber or Virgin?
- Compound words. Evernote or FaceTime are great examples of when words are smushed together but still make sense.
- Mashed-up names: Instagram* being an example of a famous brand that's done this.
- Suffixes like -ify, -ster or -ly added to words – think Spotify or Deliveroo.
- Vowels can sometimes be removed – Flickr has managed to do this and, because of the confidence in their marketing, it doesn't appear to be strange.

You might also consider using your own name as the name of your business. This can be done very effectively if you are at the centre of your business, especially if you are a service provider.

It's something that I've done in my company, Design Jessica. I kept it to my first name only as I knew I would be changing my surname when I married but you could choose either name or even your middle name(s). You might even want to include your maiden name, if you have one, or any of your children's and pet's names. The lovely Susannah at Rose & The Wildflowers named her business after her little girl, who inspires her to keep going every day. It's your business, so make sure you explore all of these ideas.

Write any new ideas that pop up below.

By now, you should have a good idea of your new business name. Write it below in all its glory!

Take some time to step back and look at your new name. But here's the most important thing... Do you love it? You'll be looking at that name a lot so make sure you do. It sure is going to be on a lot of things moving forward!

TIP: Once you've chosen your new name, avoid asking too many people what they think. I know you might think that a lot of opinions might be the best way to decide if it's okay, but the reality is that the people you're speaking to haven't gone to the same level of research as you have and probably don't know you or your product/service as well. You might think that, if they are in your target audience, they would know best, but the reality is that the more opinions you get, the more confused you will become.

Although it's good to get input from your future clients and customers, too many chefs spoil the broth! If you aren't 100% sure about your new name, maybe select some well-trusted friends or family members to help you get some new ideas together. You could even run through the naming activity above with them for extra help?

Finally, before you announce your wonderful new business name to the world, you'll want to make sure that it's not already being used somewhere else and is available for you to purchase as a website domain. For once, Google is your friend here, so take some time to research the name online to make sure it's not already taken or trademarked. You can head to Companies House to check but Facebook can be a great search engine for this, too.

Now that you have your shiny new business name (and you know that you can legally use it!), it's time to 'claim' it so that others can't. You can do this in a few different ways and you should pick the option(s) most suitable for you. Remember, like all things in this book, you can pick and choose what fits you best.

'CLAIMING' YOUR NEW BUSINESS NAME

- *Limited company incorporation* – The added bonus of registering your business as a limited company is that you now claim your business name. It means that no other business can trade with the same name within the UK. Having this type of business means that, should anyone else try to operate using your name, you can approach them and get them to stop trading with your business name. However, a limited company does come with some added legal responsibilities, which have been outlined in the next section.

- *Trademarking and registered trademark* – You must have spotted the little ™ and the ® on certain logos and straplines? These have been registered by the business owner(s) with the Intellectual Property Office of the United Kingdom so that no one else can use them commercially. It's something I have done with both Milspo® and *The InDependent Spouse*®. Both of these are registered trademarks and owned by me, which is why I can add the ® just after them. Before they were officially registered and added to the Intellectual Property Office (IPO) register, I could use the ™ to show that the trademark belonged to me and that it was in the process of being registered. This process isn't wholly fallible, as you still need to defend your ™ and ®, but it makes it all a lot easier to own your name and, subsequently, your brand. Similar to incorporating as a limited company, it's also recognised legally.

- *Social media and website* – The most straightforward way to 'claim' your name is simply getting it out there. Once you know you can use it legally and commercially, you should purchase your chosen business name in domain form and any variants you think might be necessary. For example, for my design business, Design Jessica, I have previously purchased www.designjessica.co.uk for my main site, but also www.designjessica.com and www.design-jessica.co.uk. This helps stop your clients and customers from being confused should they accidentally type in your web address incorrectly and find themselves on the wrong website. You can also get these additional domains to reroute to your main website.

You should also start setting up your social media profiles with your new business name – don't forget to keep the name choice consistent so that your clients and customers can find you. Remember, this book isn't going to talk you through the details of how to set up your social media accounts as this information changes with every update. Helpful videos on how to set them up are most often provided by each of the social media companies themselves. However, you should be aware that just setting up social media accounts in your business name doesn't cover you legally and that others can trade under the same name as you. You could also be asked to change your name if it's subsequently registered or used as a limited company in the future.

TIP: Naming your business is exciting but there are a few things that you simply cannot do as a business owner. Certain words – many of them medical but also words such as 'Olympic' or 'Architect' – are protected in the UK and their use for a company name could be a criminal offence. Head to Companies House to make sure you aren't breaking any laws.

IT'S TIME TO REGISTER WITH HMRC

HMRC (His Majesty's Revenue & Customs) requires you to tell them of your earnings in your business. They'll be asking you to declare your income so that you can be assessed on how much tax and National Insurance you will need to pay. Contributing to the economy is something we are all responsible for and something we should be proud to do, especially if we have earned it through our own business.

All new business owners will need to register to fill out some sort of annual tax assessment and some may also choose to register their business as a limited company. There are also other types of business set up, with partnerships, charities and community interest companies (CICs) being some of the most common examples but are not that widely used. If you are considering setting up one of these, you should seek financial advice first.

Here's my brief overview of the two most common types of business but I would recommend you visit www.gov.uk for further information.

What is a sole trader?

A sole trader is essentially a self-employed person who is the sole owner of their business. It's the simplest business structure out there, which is probably why it's the most popular. It's easy to set up with minimal paperwork – except for the annual self assessment tax return. It's also a bit more private than a limited company as the details can't be found via Companies House.

The disadvantages of operating as a sole trader is that the government considers the business and the owner as the same entity. If the business accrues debt, so does the owner. The tax level also increases less beneficially in comparison with a limited company so, at a certain point in their business, a sole trader may decide to change to a limited company.

What is a limited company?

A limited company is a type of business structure with its own legal identity that is separate from its owners (shareholders) and its managers (directors). This remains the case even if it's run by just one person acting as both a shareholder and a director. This means that, unlike a sole trader, any debt accrued stays with the business and doesn't affect the director's assets. Limited companies also pay corporation tax, rather than income tax, which can be more favourable. And, once registered as a limited company, no one else can use your business name unlike sole traders who don't have the same legal protection.

However, with the limited company registration comes a whole host of responsibilities including, but not limited to, the yearly annual return, as well as completing annual accounts and legal registrations. You'll also need to pay a fee to incorporate as a limited company and spend time keeping things up to date with HMRC and the responsibilities they require you to carry out.

Ultimately, it's important to weigh up the difference between a sole trader and a limited company, as the structure you choose could have an impact on everything from profits to paperwork. Don't rush into any decisions and speak to an accountant or seek business advice if you're unsure, as their expertise can be invaluable when it comes to the tax facts.

It's up to you to pick whichever legal setup fits you and your new business best. But don't let the thought of tax and the formality of HMRC get to you. It can be overwhelming at first but there is a load of support out there to help you. Don't let that uncomfortable feeling stand in the way of your dreams.

Remember: 'This negative voice in my head isn't my truth.
*I **can** do this, and I **will** do this – **just watch me go!**'*

ACCOUNTING AND BOOKKEEPING

As well as registering with HMRC, you will need to start keeping track of your expenses and income to complete your returns. There are literally hundreds of accounting apps and websites that can help you with your business accounts or you can simply keep a spreadsheet with the details – you just need to make sure that you back it up as you'll need to keep records for at least five years after the 31 January submission deadline of the relevant tax year.

Do some research and ask other business owners what they recommend and how they do their accounting. Either way, just make sure you keep a record of what you are spending and earning. There's nothing worse than getting to the end of your financial year and not having accurate records. Not only could you end up paying too much tax but you could also be stung with an audit. It's better to keep a record of everything right from the start and update it as you go.

ASK PERMISSION

I think we can all agree that one of the weirder parts of military life is living in a military married quarter or Service Family Accommodation (SFA). If you do, you will need to ask permission from the contractor that manages your house or, if you are renting privately, you'll need to get permission from your landlord. Historically, you'd also need to gain consent from your partner's chain of command (yes, I know!), but this varies from base to base, so be sure to ask your local welfare office as they are the ones who will be up to date with the policies. There's usually a form that needs to be filled out. Annoyingly, at the time of writing this book, it was decided that the permission needs to be applied for at the start of each posting... another thing to add to that moving list.

INSURANCES

Business insurance, like any insurance, is a must if you want to be covered for when things might not go to plan in your business. You can get insurance to cover all elements of your business, from injury and cyber-attack to income loss as a result of illness. They are all different at varying price points so you should consider talking to a broker or an insurance expert about what would suit your business best. Insurance is something that you might never have to claim, but the reality of not having it when you need it could be devastating for you and your company.

Okay, so that chapter felt a little bit more 'serious' than the last few but, I promise, all of this hard work and effort you've made on the foundations of your business will set you up for success for years to come. Doing these important tasks first means that you won't get into trouble or have to make expensive changes to your business later on down the line.

These are my six most important things to do as a first step in getting going and, In the next chapter, I'll be giving you some things to think about that will get you ready for the launch of your business. But, before we move on, just take a moment to congratulate yourself. It's been a challenging chapter but you've made some great plans and you now have the start of a fantastic business. It has strong foundations, an amazing name, is legal in the eyes of the government** (and, weirdly, the MOD) and you are one step closer to launching your dream business. **Well done, you! I am so excited to see what you do next.**

Did you know, the name Instagram is an amalgamation of 'instant camera' and 'telegram'? You're welcome.

**But, do look deeper into regulations if you are creating a food product business, or anything within the beauty industry. These are regulated. You should also do your research if you are a service-based industry offering advice and consultancy, as you may need to register with a government or industry body if they are regulated.

7

THE NEXT LEVEL
OF BUSINESS BUILDING

"A big business starts small."

– Sir Richard Branson. English business magnate, investor and author

Okay. You should now have all the elements you need to kick-start and launch your posting-proof business. How exciting! But, as you might expect, there's so much more to it than just the legal stuff. So, over the next few pages, I will run you through some more business details that you might want to consider working on next.

TIP: There will be a lot of detail coming up, which will cover the kinds of things you can do to get your business launched successfully. If you are like me, you'll undoubtedly think that the busier you are with planning and scheduling, the more you are doing to grow your business. However, sometimes filling your time with tasks that could probably wait a little longer might just be an attempt to procrastinate because you're a little bit too worried about taking that big step in actually launching.

Just remember our mantra…

'This negative voice in my head isn't my truth.

I can do this and I will do this – just watch me go!'

Now is the time to step back and make sure you are planning things that will benefit your business journey, rather than creating 'to-dos' that are, in fact, just roadblocks stopping you from getting where you want to go. Make sure you're being honest with yourself and keep that in mind...

First up, it's time to think about launching!

Together, in the exercises below, we're going to work out what you might want to do before you launch. We'll also be giving each task a score to one to ten based on the importance of each task. This will help you to work out if it REALLY needs to be achieved before you launch or whether you're perhaps slipping into a little bit of procrastination.

SETTING A LAUNCH DATE – SCORE   /10

At this point, you should be ready to set the date in which you are planning to officially open your business and launch yourself into the world of self-employment. Setting a launch date gives you something to work towards but, more importantly, a date that you can work back from.

If you have a date to work back from, you can decide what's possible and can be done in the time frame you have. Remember, you don't want to put off launching for too long but you also want to make sure you give yourself as much chance of success as possible.

So, here we go. The BIG question. When would you like to start your business?

DATE:

Now, write down specifically why you have picked this date:

WHERE ARE YOU GOING TO WORK? – SCORE   /10

Oh, I love this part! Let's talk about working spaces.

No matter what you do for a business, you will need your own space to do it in. Believe me, it's really important; especially when working from home, which you most likely will do no matter what business you have.

You might think you can work from a kitchen table and clear everything away each night. Or, maybe, you may choose to work from a co-working or hot-desking space but, trust me, tidying away every time is going to become tedious. Before you know it, you'll be eating your meals off your lap or simply not showing up to your shared office whilst your work takes over your home.

Even if you find yourself in the teeniest married quarter or home, you need to find some space that is yours to work in. Not only will it save you having to clear work away every night, but it will also give you somewhere that you can be inspired, stay focused and have just for you.

At the very minimum, in this space you will need a comfy, supportive chair and a desk. It doesn't need to be a vast desk if you haven't got the space but it does need to be practical. You will be there for a lot of hours so make sure you are comfy in where you are sat – no one needs a crocked back!

If you do have space or even your own room (spare bedrooms are perfect for this in a married quarter and your guests really won't mind sleeping in your lovely office when they stay over) you'll want it to be beautiful and reflective of you. You should think about lighting, storage and layout, as well as the sort of work you are doing. I personally love a framed inspirational quote on my office wall and I always make sure that I have my key reasons for running my business pinned to a board near my Mac. And, if you've been to any of my online webinars or virtual networking sessions, you'll know that I even have a felt swan on my wall – for no specific reason except the fact that I love it and it makes me happy. It's my space and I want it to be as creative as possible.

Even if you have a physical shop or your work means that you won't be working from home full-time, you'll still end up doing some work in your home, so make sure it's lovely and is a dedicated space just for you.

Think about a space in your home that you could dedicate to becoming your office. Is it practical? Is it light enough? Can you focus there?

Now, make a list of everything you will NEED in order for it to become a great office space.

TIP: Remember, these are classed as business expenses so keep your receipts if you have to buy anything. Charity shops are an excellent place to source furniture if you are just starting out and want to save the funds for other parts of your business.

…and now, what else might you quite like to add in there – make it fun!

DECIDING ON YOUR PRODUCTS AND SETTING YOUR PRICES – SCORE /10

In chapter 5, you figured out the sort of industry you will be in and you had a little look at the competitors you will have. Now it's time to get laser-focused on the products or services you will be providing for your clients and how much they will cost.

There are entire books out there solely dedicated to picking the correct pricing structure and it's one of those things that evolves alongside your business. So, instead of writing pages and pages on pricing, I want to take you through a little exercise I do when I am deciding what to charge for my services (there's a second exercise if you are running a product-based business).

However, as you can probably guess, there isn't a set equation when it comes to working out your pricing. Remember that Victoria Beckham T-shirt we talked about in chapter 5? As with everything in this book you should also add your opinions and the research you have about your industry as you go along. But, as well as this, now is a great time to think about pricing. You'd be amazed at how many of us have under-priced ourselves or not ever really considered what to charge.

SERVICE BUSINESS PRICING

If you are a service-based provider (as in you provide clients with a service in which you usually, but not exclusively, charge by the hour rather than a product with a fixed price), you will probably want to start off by working out your hourly rate. That's the rate that you charge your clients for the services they require. This is a great baseline that will help you work out what to quote for each job. To figure this out, you will need to research what others might be charging, the experience you have and the money you need to earn in order to make your business viable.

Here's an equation that's commonly used at this time to find your hourly rate:

$$\frac{Desired\ profit\ amount\ +\ desired\ salary\ +\ operating\ costs}{Annual\ income\text{-}producing\ hours}$$

- *Desired profit amount:* usually in the first year, all profits are reinvested into the company.
- *Desired salary:* it's essential that you pay yourself for the work that you do in your business. You can take this as drawings if you're a sole trader or as dividends if you are a director of a limited company.
- *Operating costs:* these are the costs that are incurred as a result of running your business.
- *Annual income-producing hours:* these are the number of hours you will want to or can work in any given year.

Here's an example that will hopefully make this a little easier to understand.

You would like to make £5,000 profit this year to re-invest in your business next year and you would like to pay yourself a salary from your business of £25,000. It costs approximately £10,000 for you to run your business and, once you have factored in your holidays, post-deployment leave and bank holidays, you estimate that you will be working for roughly 45 weeks of the year.

It's important to remember to also deduct the hours you will spend completing your admin and any non-billable hours that you can't charge your clients for, which brings the income-producing hours down to around 40 weeks.

If you were to work six hours a day, this would equal 30 hours a week (on the presumption that you will be working five days a week). When this is multiplied by 40 (the number of weeks you predict you will be working), that makes 1,200 hours a year.

I hope you're still with me on this…

Placing these figures into the equation above looks something like this:

$$\frac{£5,000 + £25,000 + £10,000}{1,200 \text{ HOURS}} = £33.33 \text{ PER HOUR}$$

However, I personally have a slightly different way in which I price my services and that will also be the same way that you would generate the prices for your products.

In my design business, I offer packages at different price points. This includes a starting, basic priced package; a medium-priced package; and a super-shiny package. These are my top three most requested product design quotes and, in the long run, it helps to speed up the process of people commissioning designs from me.

USE THIS SPACE TO WORK OUT YOUR HOURLY RATE.
TIP: I also publish my prices on my website as it helps weed out those clients who either can't afford my services or believe that I am too cheap (some people will always prefer to have that expensive white Victoria Beckham T-shirt). This simple addition to my website saves me so much time. Usually, by the time a client has got in touch with me, they know the sort of quote to expect and I don't spend my days replying to the wrong type of client.

PRODUCT BUSINESS PRICING

If you are building a product-based business, first and foremost, you need to understand all of the costs involved in getting each product out of the door and into your customers' hands.

When you produce physical products, you'll need to firstly look at all of the raw materials you use to make the final product. How much does that bundle (which includes every element needed to make your product) cost and how many products can you create from each material bundle? This will give you a rough estimate of your cost of goods sold per item. You should also be adding your hourly rate to that. These are classed as your variable costs since they can vary from month to month.

Next, you'll need to add a profit margin to your pricing. Let's say for example that you want to earn a 20% profit margin on your products, on top of your variable costs. When you're choosing this percentage, it's important to remember two things:

1. You haven't yet included your fixed costs, so you will have costs to cover beyond just your variable costs.
2. You need to consider the overall market and ensure that your price (including this margin) still falls within the overall "acceptable" price for your market. For example, if you're twice the price of all your competitors, you might find making a sale pretty difficult depending on your product category.

Fixed costs are the costs that you'd pay no matter what – those that stay the same whether you sell ten products or ten million products. Just like a service-based business, these costs need to be included if you're going to charge appropriately. You need to work out how many products you need to sell to break even.

Okay, so let's say you're producing teddy bears.

It costs £25 for the raw materials to make ten bears – that's £2.50 a bear. You want to be paid £20 an hour and within those 60 minutes, you can make two bears. As it stands, that makes the variable costs £12.50 per bear.

You know you can charge £20 per bear by looking at your competitors.

The total price of £20 per bear includes your hourly rate, all variable costs and the remainder (£7.50) can go towards your fixed costs.

Your fixed costs are £5,000. So, to cover these, you need to work out how many bears you need to make and sell to afford the fixed costs of £5,000.

It's okay – you don't need to get your calculators out. I've got you!

To cover these costs, you'd need to make and sell 667 teddy bears in a year.

Can you feasibly sell 667 bears in a year? Does your price work with others in your industry? Do you need to amend your profit margins?

You should be going through this process with every single product you make to help you decide whether they are viable products for your business and whether you want to stock them based on these prices. As long as your price covers your expenses and provides you with some profit, you can test and amend as you go.

Whichever price you come up with, the choices you make now are not carved into concrete – they're just as flexible as your business. You'll want to adjust your pricing regularly to reflect your experience and costs to produce changes. You should be reviewing your pricing every six months.

BRANDING IN YOUR BUSINESS – SCORE   /10

Branding in your business is very exciting. For me, as a designer, it means all of the 'pretty stuff' – your logo, your colours, your font choices – but, for you, it should also include your tone of voice when you're writing anything, your business's place in the market (again, another mention of that famous T-shirt) and everything associated with the outward facing parts of your business.

> *"Your brand is what other people say about you when you're not in the room."*
>
> *– Jeff Bezos. American internet entrepreneur, industrialist, media proprietor and investor, founder of Amazon*

Branding really is a subject I could write a whole book on! It is my specialist subject and what I love to spend my days doing. Because I want you to make the most of your branding in your business (and to save diluting this chapter), I've included a bonus chapter at the end of this book. It's more detailed than the previous activities and runs through everything you should consider if you're creating your own branding. Even if you're not doing it yourself, it is an excellent source of info if you're commissioning a designer instead.

What I will say now is that the most important thing about your branding is consistency! Everything you produce in your business that's sent out into the world is part of your brand. People are fundamentally lazy and busy so don't make it too difficult for your clients to find you or recognise you straight away. Instead, make sure you have a clear and consistent output that's quickly recognised and memorable.

YOUR SHOP FRONT – SCORE   /10

A considerable part of your brand and how people feel about your business is based on your shop front – be that a real bricks and mortar one or a digital one.

If you don't have a website for your business in this digital age, I'm sorry to say that you don't really exist. Your website is the first port of call for the majority of your audience; something that was highlighted when the pandemic struck.

Websites (and building them) can seem overwhelming but you may be pleasantly surprised by the variety of support that is out there. For example, many website-building platforms have their own online videos and live chats with developers who can talk you through much of what you might want to create for your business. And of course, like the design, you can commission your own developer to build a website just for your business. These can range from simple templates that you can populate with your own information or they can be 100% bespoke and coded to your needs – the price will, of course, reflect this.

As part of purchasing a domain, you will often get email addresses with it too. For example, when I bought www.milspo.co.uk, I was given access to the hello@milspo.co.uk email address. You should always consider using that business email address when doing anything to do with your business. It makes you look a bit more polished and professional.

A website is essential to your business and is one of the things I would seriously recommend you putting at the top of your list for the first few months of your start-up.

Remember though, your first ever website will evolve as you and your business grow, and just having an online presence (even if it's not perfect) is a thousand times better than not having anything there at all.

TIP: Don't forget, your clients are busy people and they'll give up if your website is too challenging to use. You should be testing your website on your friends and family and asking for constructive feedback on its usability. What I find helpful is sitting with a customer or a client as they first view your new site to find out what they like and what they struggle with. You might assume that everything will work first time but seeing your site being used in real life by someone who is unfamiliar with it will give you a whole new view on how it works. You can also download apps that give you a heat map of where and when your users are scrolling, clicking and ignoring. This is something that can help you put your key information in the perfect place.

You might already have been selling online via your social media accounts but it's worth remembering that you don't own those sites. What would happen to your business if Facebook or Instagram simply disappeared one day or decided that selling through their platform was no longer allowed? Having your own website gives you ownership of your shop and how people can find you.

Which brings me nicely to list building.

EMAIL LISTS – SCORE   /10

Imagine if one day you found that your favourite social media channel had fallen offline. How would your clients and customers find you? That's where an email list comes in.

An email list is quite literally a list of email addresses from people who have chosen to sign up to hear more information from you about your business. They've usually opted to sign up because you've offered them something in exchange for their email address. This could be a discount code, a free downloadable or the offer of a one-to-one consultation. That's called a lead magnet.

Since the General Data Protection Regulation (GDPR) came into effect in April 2016, you can no longer legally add any email address from someone residing in Europe to your list without obtaining the owner's consent. This is the case for wherever you are in the world.

GDPR can be confusing. Luckily, most of the best-known email list building software developers have a built-in response to this and there are step-by-step videos on their sites that walk you through what you need to know. So, it's nothing to worry about – just be aware that GDPR exists and that you need to comply with the rules. Like all things in business, it's best to do your research.

You will also need to be aware of how to protect this data by considering activating two-factor authentication (2FA), also referred to as two-step verification or dual-factor authentication, to your computer or where your client's details are stored. This system is a security process in which users provide two different authentication factors to verify themselves. This process is in place to better protect both the user's credentials and the resources the user can access.

It's so important to keep your data safe and the Information Commissioner's Office (ICO) has a lot of online help around this. You will also need to register with the ICO and, in the majority of cases, pay an annual fee to them. The ICO has a handy questionnaire that you can fill out on their website to help you with this.

But, don't panic too much. It's all very well supported and most of these sites have chat functions that you can ask questions on should you need any help.

Having an established email list is great for business. With the way in which social media focuses so heavily now on algorithms, it's becoming more difficult to get in front of your ideal clients. By having an email list, you have been invited to drop directly into their inboxes whenever you like.

But, to get them signed up in the first place, you'll need a snazzy lead magnet.

SETTING YOUR WORKING HOURS (AND TAKING TIME OFF)
– SCORE   /10

There's no doubt that one of the key reasons you listed previously for starting your own business is flexibility. The best part of self-employment is that you no longer need to work the 9-to-5 – you can choose your working hours! But just because you *can* work whenever you can, doesn't mean you should.

You should always have set 'opening' times for your business. These are the times in which you will be available for your clients and customers to approach and work with you. These hours should work for you, not the other way around! It will be clear when you are open if you have a bricks and mortar shop but, don't forget, you'll also need to factor in the hours that you'll spend working on all the other parts of your business.

What's also completely epic about running your own business is that you get to decide when you take time off, too! So you don't have to stick to the regular 28 days' holiday that you usually get with employment.

TIP: Invest in a good yearly calendar. I have one that I stick on my office wall. On my calendar, I block out when I can't or don't want to work in my business. For me, that's days like my birthday, Christmas, bank holidays and, of course, weekends. After that, I block out any holiday I would like to take and, of course, schedule the inevitable moves with postings (with at least a week on either side as a buffer). You might also consider dates you want to take off for your family, such as school holidays, inset days, school sports days and deployment return dates. Remember, you are your own boss, so you get to pick when you take time off work.

By seeing the whole year set out in front of you and the availability you have to work, you can plan precisely what you want to do. This will help give you the flexibility to fit in everything you want to.

In the space below, make a list of the types of time off you want and give yourself a rough idea of how many days that is per year. Not only will it give you an idea of what you can achieve, it'll also help you with the costing exercises we worked through before.

You should already have a fair idea of the hours of the day you want to work. After all, you don't have to start at 9am and finish at 5pm (especially useful if you have a school run to fit in), but you should take into consideration the hours that your clients or customers would be expecting you to work as well. Of course, if you're posted abroad and your clients are here in the UK, you might also need to apply adapted working hours to fit in with them. Generally, as long as you're clear and let everyone know your working hours, there should be very little confusion.

TIP: Write your working hours in your email signature, especially if they're not the usual 9-to-5.

A huge part of running a successful business is creating content. This can be for anything from your social media posts or video, to a podcast or a blog series, but the main reason for creating this free content is to show the world that you've arrived and you are the expert.

So, at this point you might be saying to yourself: '*But Jess, creating FREE content? Surely that's going to take time and effort when I should be doing the things that make me money. Plus, it's free – I should be charging for it.*'

Here's the thing.

For your perfect customer to part with their hard-earned cash and believe in your product or service, it's going to take more than a good idea. First, you need to prove to them that you are the bee's knees! Then, you need to show them that not only are you an expert with what you do but that what you provide is a thousand times better than what they can find anywhere else and that they can't possibly live without it. It's basic capitalism – your customers and clients NEED to work with you and you need to show them why. This is the key to your business achieving the success it deserves.

You want your clients and customers to get hooked on what you do and how you do it, and the best way to do this is to dazzle them! So, alongside your amazing email lead magnet, you will want to be thinking about the other things you could create to get your name front and centre in their brains.

Remember that it should reflect your brand, be informative yet not too salesy and be attractive to entice your audience. Most importantly, you should enjoy creating it. The more you enjoy it, the more your clients will too, and they'll be chomping at the bit to work with you.

The last thing, before we move onto the next chapter, that I want you to think about is celebrating.

> *"The more you praise and celebrate your life,*
> *the more there is in life to celebrate."*
> – *Oprah Winfrey. American talk show host,*
> *television producer, actor, author and philanthropist*

CELEBRATING – SCORE 10/10 (LET ME FILL THAT ONE OUT FOR YOU... IT'S THE BEST PART!)

Although exciting, working on your business can sometimes be a bit all-encompassing and it can be so easy for you to forget to stop and celebrate. The first and most important celebration that you need to do is on your launch day.

This is the first OFFICIAL day of your new business. A business that is going to change your outlook on life. A business that will test you, challenge you, knock you down and build you up. You will want to mark this in a special way, so make sure you do.

If you are already at the launch stage of your new business, then you are due some serious pats on the back! You have come so far and you should be so proud of all that you have achieved. It's not easy setting everything up for launch day but you got there. I am so excited to see your shiny new business become a huge success!

———

Whoa!? That was an EPIC chapter but I felt that it would be a good idea to give you a taste of some of my best business learnings for starting a business and, even if you don't manage to do all of these before you launch, they will be a great resource to return to as your business grows

In the next part of the book, I'll be working through mindset and exploring how the way you think can dramatically help you stay fighting fit in business. It's going to make a real difference to all that you do.

But, in the meantime, take a little moment to stop, congratulate yourself and feel proud of your new business. **You have created something amazing!**

8

BONUS CHAPTER – THINGS YOU MIGHT EXPERIENCE IN THE FIRST FEW MONTHS

Even though you're ready to launch (and, of course, celebrate that amazing day), before we leave this stage, I just want to share with you a few more points that will help you in the next few months and years of business growth.

You might find your business coming across a few stumbling blocks, challenges and maybe even some growing pains. So, here are some things that might be useful to read now as well as revisit when you come up against them.

First up, I want you to consider how you're going to build your network. The real strength of any business comes from the network it has and the best way to grow as a business owner is to surround yourself with people who keep you inspired.

NETWORKING

When you think of networking, what might jump into your head is a grotty old conference room full of grey men in suits or (post-pandemic) a dull Zoom room with one person hogging the space and talking nonsense – it's enough to put anyone off! If that's all you've experienced, I wouldn't be surprised if you told me that you never wanted to try it again but, believe me when I say, there's SO much more to networking than this.

Networking, both in real life and online, is crucial to your business's success for so many more reasons than just making a sale. For example:

- It allows you to connect with those you might need business help from.
- It allows you to offer your business speciality to an extended network.
- *'People buy from people'*, so you are far more likely to sell to someone who knows you.
- You can learn a lot from other business owners.
- You get business support when you need it and not just for outsourcing.
- You can make real friendships!

TIPS: Things to remember when you are networking:

1. *Smile! It will make a massive difference to how you feel. Just making a physical change to your body can convince your brain that you are doing okay and it'll also help others know that you are lovely. Everything is always easier with a smile on your face.*

2. *Remember that everyone is doing their best. Honestly, they will be just as worried as you about making a mistake or not saying the right thing, so be gentle with them.*

3. *You need to turn up more than once. I have lost count of the number of business owners who have told me that they no longer go to networking because they went once and never got any*

business from it. Commitment is key to networking as well as building trust and a meaningful connection with the people you meet. That doesn't happen after just one meeting. But, if you turn up a few times and get to know everyone else there, you'll find that you build a connection, especially with those who want to work with you. Remember, 'people buy from people'.

4. *Not everyone will get what you do and that's okay. Even with the best will in the world, not everyone will be your ideal customer, which isn't all bad. However, don't write these people off straight away. I've found that even though you may not be made for each other, I bet these people know a lot of people who are. It's all about leveraging their extended network. They can become a cheerleader for your business when someone they know might need your products or services. It's a great way of spreading your offering even further.*

5. *It will be worth it in the end. I promise that investing time and money in networking can make a massive difference to your business success and, even though it might be uncomfortable at the start, you will soon find all that effort is worth it once your business begins to grow.*

"The currency of real networking is not greed but generosity."

– Keith Ferrazzi. American author and entrepreneur

BUILDING A TRANSIENT NETWORK

Networking isn't just something that happens at organised events. The secret to making the most of any connection is the work you do around those events that is entirely separate from them. You can build a network at any time; one that can travel with you no matter where you are posted.

To do this away from organised events, show up where your audience is and offer them support. This could be in person, online in Facebook groups or on Zoom meetups. Be there to offer your advice and you'll soon be known as the expert and the one to go to when anyone needs help in your industry.

You'll also want to turn up as your genuine self – 'people buy from people'! It's easy to get wrapped up in the world of 'success' and 'faking it until you make it', but actually, if you want to attract your ideal clients and customers, you should consider being your genuine self as much as you can. After all, putting all that effort into pretending to be someone else is exhausting. Meanwhile, your ideal client has wandered past.

'Do not bring people in your life who weigh you down, and trust your instincts. Good relationships feel good. They feel right. They don't hurt. They're not painful. That's not just with somebody you want to marry, but it's with the friends you choose.'

It's with the people you surround yourself with."

– Michelle Obama. American attorney, author and former First Lady of the US

HOW TO LEVERAGE THE STRENGTH OF YOUR NETWORK

Building a network does take some work but it will make a massive difference to your business's speed of success. So here's a little exercise on how to do it quickly and successfully using the people you already know.

List anyone you can think of who might be able to help you grow your business.

List anyone you've met before who you would like to reconnect with.

List everyone you might not necessarily be connected with but who inspire you.

Now the exciting part! It's time to connect.

Contact those listed and ask them if they would like to connect and talk about business. It really is that simple!

Ideally, you'll want to schedule an hour-long one-to-one with them in order to get to know them and their business a little better.

You'll want to spend about 30 minutes talking about each of your businesses and genuinely listening to each other.
You should ask sensible questions and suggest people you

know that you could connect them with to help their business grow. You should make notes and keep in mind their call to actions (what they are asking of you) so that you can action them after the meeting. Genuinely get to know them – you never know when that connection could be useful.

I want to tell you a little story, which has been passed on from one of my previous networking groups. One day Sarah (who sold those big knickers that hold everything in... you know the ones) met up with Julia, who she'd met at a networking group. Julia made high-end aromatherapy candles that helped new mothers stay calm. Although they got on, they could never really work out exactly how they could help each other take their business to the next level – after all, there are only so many pairs of pants and candles two women can buy! But, as they got talking, Sarah mentioned in passing that she would love to see the singer Adele in her very special pants. And you'll never guess what... Julia's sister just happened to be Adele's personal assistant! Now, I am pretty sure this story is just myth that has been embellished over time (so please don't sue me, Adele!), but, even if it is, it's a great example of how an extended network works. You never really know who you're talking to and, especially within our community, who they might be married to. Just because you don't think that person can work for your business, it doesn't mean there's not some way in which they can help you or vice versa, so what's to lose?

It's all about building a network, so make sure you really get to know each other and think about how you can help each other with your respective extended networks. It's not just about them buying from you – it's not a sales pitch meeting – it's about connecting.

And don't forget, business owners always want to help each other, so be brave and send that invite to connect!

BUSINESS MENTORS

*"A mentor is someone who
allows you to see the hope inside yourself."*

*— Oprah Winfrey. American talk show host, television producer, actor,
author and philanthropist*

Another handy tool that can help you when you are more established, is having a business mentor.

The term mentor comes from Greek mythology. When Odysseus left for the Trojan War, he asked his friend 'Mentor' to take care of his son, Telemachus. Mentor became the boy's teacher, coach, adviser and counsel. Every day's a school day!

But nowadays, away from Greek mythology, a business mentor is someone with business experience who can teach, guide and help you explore all possible options and is a trusted adviser in all aspects of business.

A mentor is usually someone who has experience in your field and can take the form of either a paid mentor or a volunteer mentor. The joy of a mentor is that you can tap into the experience they have and learn from their mistakes (without making costly mistakes of your own) – they'll even help to hold you accountable for things.

The secret here is that you get on well with one another, so make sure you have some preliminary calls before you settle on a particular mentor.

BUSINESS COACH

A business coach is usually someone who will help you to achieve an objective based on the needs of your business. They are normally paid to do so.

The difference between a mentor and a coach is that a business mentor will use their experience to help and guide you, whereas a business coach will use your expertise to create a path for you to follow. A business coach may not have the same level of all-round business experience as a business mentor but is usually qualified in coaching and a real asset to your business.

I have used both coaches and mentors in the past and both have offered so much to my business. If you're serious about success, you should really consider working with a coach or a mentor.

BUILDING YOUR TEAM

"Great things in business are never done by one person; they're done by a team of people."

– Steve Jobs. American business magnate, industrial designer, investor and media proprietor

At some point, very soon, you're going to experience some growth and (unfortunately yet inevitably) the growing pains that come with it. You will get to a point in your business when you can no longer do it all, so you'll want to start growing your team and outsourcing some of the things you no longer have the time to do.

Here are some of the red flags you might notice that are letting you know that it's time to start outsourcing:
1. You're overly stressed – time to send out some of those tasks.
2. You are spending your time on jobs you can't stand. Entrepreneurship is tough, so best not to spend your energy suffering through the jobs you hate.
3. Your customers aren't receiving the attention they had previously, which is REALLY bad for business.
4. You no longer have time to brainstorm or plan in your business,

which is slowing down your growth.
5. An area of your business has been ignored for too long. Maybe you've not done your accounts for months or your social media has been abandoned because you lack time – disaster!

One of the most challenging parts of owning a small business or being an entrepreneur is doing it all. In addition to growing your company and delivering for clients, you also have to wear all the other hats of a business owner. So when that becomes too much, you might turn to outsourcing. This is a big deal, and recognising when it's time to outsource is a really key point in your business's growth.

ACCOUNTING

One of the first things you're probably keen to outsource (if you're not an accountant or bookkeeper yourself) is your accounts. Since nearly everyone hates maths, bookkeeping may be a stressful time-suck that gets in the way of your primary business activities – it certainly is for me!

Luckily there's a whole industry dedicated to tax and accounting. Ensure those you approach are professional and don't forget to ask your network for recommendations. Good accountants and bookkeepers are worth their weight in gold, so do your research.

ADMIN

Whether or not your business operates online, virtual assistants (VAs) are some of the most common staff members to add to your team. They are online-based workers who do admin tasks to support your business and many have a speciality focus, such as social media management.

DESIGN

If you have little or no experience with graphic or web design, don't try to teach yourself from scratch – it will just add to your time pressures. Plus, there are people like me who are qualified and can do it for you in half the time, giving you space to work on your business.

It's great to know design basics but leave the hard stuff to the professionals who will be able to do a better job at a much faster pace. You might also want to consider outsourcing your photography and video creation to experts, too. Either way, don't forget the bonus branding chapter found at the back of this book, which will help you find your perfect designer.

MARKETING

When you're up to your eyes in client work, there's a considerable chance your marketing will end up falling off your to-do list. After all, you have client work – why would you need more? Because, my dear friend, the good times won't last, especially if you're not focused on bringing in new clients. Things could get quiet very quickly!

Luckily, you can outsource your marketing, too! This could include your email marketing (using your unique lead magnet and growing email list), website search engine optimisation (SEO) so that clients find you easily, public relations (PR) specialists who use media to spread the word about your business, blog management, plus so much more! Of course, you could ask your VA to help with this, but, eventually, you'll want to talk to someone who specialises in it.

WRITING

Who doesn't love a wordsmith? If your business isn't about writing, then you shouldn't need to spend your time trying to perfect everything you do that involves words (or 'copy' as the industry calls it) – simples! There are lots of different types of word wizards to choose from. There are copywriters, who focus on creating copy for the sole purpose of advertising or marketing; there are content writers, who specialise in creating long-form, engaging content such as blog posts, newsletters and articles; there are proofreaders, who work to ensure that what you've written is free from spelling, grammar and punctuation errors; and there are also copyeditors, who not only scan your work for typos but will also double-check that everything is as readable as possible.

This means that you can outsource absolutely anything to a writer, editor or proofreader – from your social media posts and marketing materials, to your blog posts and product/service descriptions and packages. Having someone like this on your team will save you time and ensure that everything you share has a consistent tone, quality and message.

If done correctly, outsourcing can give you the space to breathe and grow your business. Yes, it's an investment but the freedom you gain means you can do what entrepreneurs do best – focus on what makes your business great.

———

So, there you have it – a few bonus bits to help support you after that initial launch stage. Although not an exhaustive list, it covers some of the areas of business that I've found people struggling with the most.

Keep referring back to these points as your business grows and try the tips and exercises in this section. But, most importantly, enjoy this growth and embrace the pains – it means you are doing something right. According to the latest figures from the Office for National Statistics (ONS), around 20% of UK companies fail within their first year, so the fact that you are here, feeling these growing pains, is a testament to your success.

Keep going!

"The greater danger
for most of us lies
not in setting our aim
too high
and falling short;
but in setting
our aim too low,
and achieving
our mark."

– Michelangelo.

Italian Renaissance sculptor, painter, architect and poet

PART TWO

CHANGING YOUR MINDSET

ADAPTING HOW YOU THINK TO BECOME
THE SUCCESSFUL BUSINESS OWNER YOU DESERVE TO BE

Oh my! How did you find Part One? I know it'll have given you the best possible start to your new business or perhaps a little refresh if you're already busy trading. By now, you should have a good idea about what you are looking to do/already doing in business and how you are going to do it or enhance it. Either way, it'll be legal, well-focused and ready for launch.

The first year of any new business is the toughest! With 20% of businesses in the UK failing within their first year and a further 60% failing within the first three years of starting up, it's not going to be an easy ride. But – *and yes, there's a wonderful 'but' (thank goodness!)* – there's a great way that you can help yourself in these first formative years: change your outlook!

The following section is all about your mindset and how adapting your outlook can help you succeed in business as well as in your personal life. I'll be talking about how I have improved my own outlook on life and business as well as sharing the stories of my amazing pals who have reaped the rewards of doing the same thing. I'll also explore the shock I felt as I transitioned from being employed to being self-employed and how I have refocused my view of my military life to help make the most I can from my life choices.

The first half of this section focuses on how you can get yourself ready to change your mindset and the steps you need to take, whereas the second half is all about how others have managed to achieve it.

Developing one's mindset has become a very popular thing to focus on over the last few years and is something I have been personally working on for many years and, actually, continue to do so to this very day. For me, it's probably one of the most important tools I use to keep me running both of my businesses with equal amounts of joy and success.

Some of the following opinions and stories might seem a little out there or, perhaps, my views might be really different from what you have experienced in this military life. Still, I am confident that each chapter will have some valuable takeaways for you and your business, so I encourage you to embrace it all, take what you need from it and apply anything that sparks interest in your world.

After all, you have nothing to lose and everything to gain!

9

"YOU ARE BRAVER THAN YOU BELIEVE, STRONGER THAN YOU SEEM, AND SMARTER THAN YOU THINK."

– a quote from Winnie the Pooh, written by A. A. Milne

One of the last questions I always ask my guests on the podcast series is: *"If you had one piece of advice for aspiring business owners, what would it be?"*. And one of the most powerful replies came from an interview I conducted in series two with Grace Selous Bull, owner of The Rainbow Tree.

*"We read a lot in our house and, since having kids, we've been rediscovering some classics. About a year ago, I came across a quote from Winnie the Pooh. I think that for anyone, it's great: '**You are braver than you believe, stronger than you seem, and smarter than you think.**' And it's so true.*

It's so easy to feel like an imposter. I should know, I suffer from it. You start to question: "What has my voice got to give?", "Who would read my book?", and "Who gave me the right to write a book?". But you really have to ignore that little inner voice and take a step of faith. Get out of the boat you're standing in and trust your worth because you are worth it. And your dreams can come true if you put in the work."

And Grace is right. Taking that leap of faith can be terrifying and starting a business can be scary. But, as Pooh said, you ARE BRAVER THAN YOU BELIEVE.

YOU ARE BRAVER THAN YOU BELIEVE

It's time to realise just how brave you are... Wait, what? You need proof? Well, you're reading this book, which shows me that: 1. you are probably thinking about starting your own business – mega brave! And, 2. you are most likely an Armed Forces partner – the bravest of them all!

Don't believe me? Just take a moment to think about it.

As military partners, we often – without much notice – wave our loved ones off to the darkest places in the world. Even if you haven't yet experienced an operational deployment, you will have at least considered that you may have to go through this at some point in your life together. And that is SO brave! Much braver than anything you will need to do in your business life and, my oh my, your business is certainly going to need you to be brave.

Believe me. Military partners make up the bravest community that I know. We rally around one another when faced with terrible stresses, unbelievable pressure and the roller coaster of Armed Forces life. We are SO brave! So, channel how epic you are, believe you are brave and let's find out how strong you are!

YOU ARE STRONGER THAN YOU SEEM

Entrepreneurship is tough! But do you know what's tougher? Military life.

Suzy Olivier runs Mothers of Enterprise – a community giving mothers the inspiration and tools to run their very own successful businesses all whilst navigating the challenges that children add to the mix.

When I spoke with Suzy in series three of the podcast, she told me: *"It's just allowing women to realise that even though the term military spouse can have a negative connotation that runs along with that, if they allow it, it can be the making of them. It can force you out of your comfort zone – and, I always say, the best things in life are outside your comfort zone.*

So, being a military spouse for me has totally made my career. It hasn't meant the death of my ambitions. It hasn't meant that I'd put my desires and goals aside when I became a wife and a mum. It's actually been the making of me. So yeah, I really would love women just to realise that if they allowed themselves to entertain thoughts outside of their norm, they might be pleasantly surprised with what they find."

Basically, if you can endure the challenges of modern military life, you are strong! So much stronger than I bet you have ever realised – the perfect recipe for building a business.

YOU ARE SMARTER THAN YOU THINK
And now, we move onto the essential part. How smart you are.

The human brain is amazing so be sure to use it for good and don't let it trick you into thinking something *can't* be done.

We are hardwired to pay more attention to the negatives than the positives.

Remember that pesky *parasympathetic nervous system* that protects you from danger? Well, it's great if you are a cavewoman but rubbish if you are starting your own business in this crazy world that we find ourselves living in today!* It means that we are hardwired to focus on negative thoughts, so it takes a lot more effort for us to get past them in order to do great things. In my case, it is so strong that I find myself on my 'spiral' – a never-ending loop that heads towards doom and gloom. That pesky system can take me from feeling absolutely fine to completely rubbish! My own brain has quite literally tricked me!

Let's take deployments as an example...

Deployments are tough and painful. So, when our very clever brains focus on the negatives, it's really hard to get out of that slump you can feel during the deployment. Of course, we miss our serving partners and sometimes we may feel frightened but, mostly, we are just pissed off. Imagine how difficult it's going to be running a business when we feel like this: *Oh, I won't do it; it'll be too hard; I won't even make any money or get any clients anyway; no one wants to work with me; I have no value; I am alone; I've never had any friends; I am entirely worthless.* Whoa, whoa, whoa! Did you see how quickly that turned? We went from finding deployment hard to feeling completely worthless. Now, you might not think like this, and this might be an extreme example, but you'll be amazed at the difference your powerful brain can make to any situation. You can do it with anything.

Something positive, perhaps. Take a holiday to the Maldives, for example: *Oh, how wonderful, I've been given a holiday to the Maldives; the beach will have white sand, the sun will be so warm, maybe too warm, will I get burnt? There will definitely be fish in the sea but I don't like fish! And there will probably be sharks, too, and what if the flight is too long or my luggage gets lost? No, I think I'll stay here, where it's safe, easy... and sort of boring.*

I have just turned down a free holiday to the Maldives because my clever brain has outsmarted me!** It sounds ridiculous but I see it so often – not the free holidays as such but most certainly the negative thinking in a seemingly positive situation!

And, to be quite honest, it still trips me up from time to time. I've lost count of the number of things I have missed out on because my brain has talked me out of it. Typically, it's because I think I am not good enough and probably quite lazy. Sometimes I genuinely believe I would be better off giving it all up, drinking coffee and just being a 'normal housewife' – whatever that may be. In reality, it's just fear surrounding the desire to achieve what I want but it manifests itself in procrastination and avoidance in working towards my goals.

But here's the thing, now that we know how clever we are and that our *parasympathetic nervous system* is just trying to look out for us, we can embrace it, amend our thinking and move forward.

Here's a little exercise I want you to complete – it's called *Dragon Slaying* and will run over the following few chapters. This exercise was first introduced to me by the amazing Canadian entrepreneur, Natalie MacNeil, and it's an adaption of a technique around limiting beliefs.

Limiting beliefs are those pesky thoughts that jump into your mind when things are going well. In the example above, they are the thoughts that stopped me from having that free trip to the Maldives. The exercise below aims to slay those negative, limiting beliefs in order to take you past the fear and towards your best life.

DRAGON SLAYING WITHIN YOUR MINDSET

First up, it's time to look those dragons in the eyes! In the space, write out all of your negative, limiting thoughts – they could be business focused or personal, or even a mixture of the two.

But, unfortunately, they generally tend to head towards the same end goal or thought – that you aren't good enough.

WHAT LIMITING BELIEFS ARE YOU CURRENTLY BATTLING?

Ooph! That was intense, wasn't it? But, by the end of this exercise, I promise you that these uncomfortable feelings will be worth sorting fairly early on as a way to get you where you deserve to be.

Next, it's time to dispel those harmful limiting beliefs – let's slay some dragons!

Pick your first limiting belief and answer the questions below. Here's an example to help you out:

My limiting belief is that I am too lazy to achieve my goals and just want to drink coffee and be a 'normal housewife' all day.

1. **How does this limiting belief affect my business?**
   I will put off deadlines, let clients down and have no repeat clients – I will make no money (proof that I am not very good at it anyway).
2. **Then what happens?**
   I will get bored and end up doing tedious work that's safe but boring. Of course, I will still socialise on a weekday rather than work but that will get boring, too – there is only so much coffee I can drink!
3. **How does that make me feel?**
   I am bored, unhappy, unfulfilled and lonely when we inevitably move home, and I will need to find a new collection of 'wives'.
4. **And again, how does that make me feel?**
   Really sad. What a waste of all my potential.
5. **And then what?**
   I will probably resent where I am posted, my husband's job and probably him as well. I feel pants! It's not going to be a good life.

Wow! Can you see how one little negative thought that I am lazy results in a sad life and an unhappy relationship? It stems from fear but it's voiced as 'proof' that I am not good enough.

Now, I want you to go through the same process for your own limiting beliefs.

WHAT IS YOUR LIMITING BELIEF?

1. How does this limiting belief affect your business?

2. Then what happens?

3. How does that make you feel?

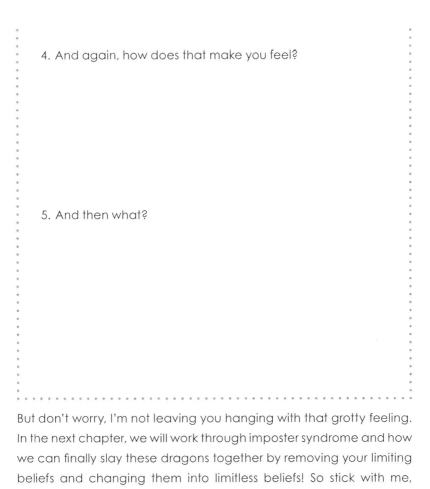

4. And again, how does that make you feel?

5. And then what?

But don't worry, I'm not leaving you hanging with that grotty feeling. In the next chapter, we will work through imposter syndrome and how we can finally slay these dragons together by removing your limiting beliefs and changing them into limitless beliefs! So stick with me, head to chapter 10 and don't let those pesky limiting beliefs ruin all of the hard work you've put in thus far!

* I obviously can't comment on how easy it was for cavewomen to set up their own businesses way back when but I'm sure they would have made it work somehow.

** FYI, this didn't actually happen in real life – I would never turn down a trip to the Maldives!

116

10

IMPOSTER SYNDROME

"She explained that many people, but especially women, feel fraudulent when they are praised for their accomplishments. Instead of feeling worthy of recognition, they feel undeserving and guilty, as if a mistake has been made. Despite being high achievers, even experts in their fields, women can't seem to shake the sense that it is only a matter of time until they are found out for who they really are–
impostors with limited skills or abilities."

– Sheryl Sandberg, Lean In: Women, Work, and the Will to Lead

Now that we've found our dragons, I want to touch briefly on imposter syndrome. There's a considerable chance that your limiting beliefs – your dragons – exist in your mind as a result of the fear of failure (we sort this out in chapter 14) or because of imposter syndrome.

Perhaps you just don't feel good enough to have your own business, or maybe you are wondering: *"How dare I even think that I can do this? I am just not good enough."*

Guess what... We all feel this way sometimes.

A few months ago, I was named by *The Telegraph* and NatWest as one of the Top UK 100 Female Entrepreneurs to Watch. I had a profile in a special eight-page supplement of the NATIONAL paper, attended a parliamentary reception at the House of Commons as part of the 100, and was a special guest at a female entrepreneurial conference held at London's British Museum. Speakers at the conference included fashionista Trinny Woodall, Jane Shepherdson from TopShop and Whistles fame, and Cambridge Satchel Company founder, Julie Deane.

Here's the thing. Up until my name was printed in that supplement, I genuinely believed they had made an admin error and accidentally emailed all who were nominated for the shortlist. So, even after getting through security at THE House of Commons, with the police monitoring and the airport-style checks, and the guest list too, I was still convinced that I wasn't meant to be there and I would be thrown out as soon as they realised. Even right up until I saw my picture on the screen at the conference, I was still convinced that they had made a mistake – or that they had perhaps felt sorry for me because I am a military wife – or, maybe, they had been short of people applying, so everyone got a place!

I mean, seriously!? The effort my brain was going to in order to make me imagine all of these things. No wonder I am tired!

On the last night of the conference, we were welcomed to a special reception in the Egyptian Sculpture Hall for posh drinks and nibbles. I had connected with a few on the 100 list over those few days and three of us were chatting about how surreal the whole thing was. In passing, I had mentioned that I thought they had made a mistake and, before I knew it, the other two had agreed and also told me about their hesitancies to believe it was real. One also didn't believe it when she got to the House of Commons and wasn't asked to leave; the other had to check her lanyard to ensure that they were, in fact, there in real life. I couldn't believe it! They felt this way, too. And, as the evening went on and the more I asked people, the more they agreed that this amazing accolade firstly didn't seem real and that they probably weren't worthy.

So, I guess what I am saying, dear reader, is that even in a room of the top 100 female entrepreneurs in the country, we still don't feel like we should be there. Can you believe it?!

This stuff is deeply rooted in our belief structure but it's when we start to notice it, shine a light on it and change our thinking that real progress can be made — so it's time to acknowledge those limiting beliefs, banish that imposter syndrome and start slaying those dragons.

"Dragons take on many forms – the hardest task of the day, a new responsibility, an impending deadline, or even dealing with conflict – and the trick is to just slay the dragon and move on. Don't overthink it. To succeed, you have to have the confidence to take things head on and keep moving forward."
– Sarah Mannone. Executive VP of Trekk

TIME TO FINALLY SLAY THOSE DRAGONS!
Those limiting beliefs from the last chapter SUCK! You are worth so much more than that. Let's banish them for good.

On the left-hand side of the next page, write down your pesky limiting belief and, on the right-hand side, write the opposite as your limitless belief.

Here's mine…

LIMITING BELIEF

My limiting belief is that I am too lazy to achieve my goals and just want to drink coffee and be a "normal" housewife.

LIMITLESS BELIEF

My limitless belief now is that I have the energy and passion I need to work at my business to become the success both it and I deserve.

LIMITING BELIEF

Your turn...

LIMITLESS BELIEF

Wow! Look at your epic set of beliefs! Can you feel the difference? It's about time you felt this good, isn't it? See how brilliant you and your business will be from now on!

Now, the key to this is you really have to believe your new limitless beliefs and they need to become soaked into your new mindset and be used daily.

We will turn these limitless beliefs into affirmations in the next chapter.

This leads us nicely into the manifesting chapter. **You are going to LOVE this one!**

11

BIGGER PICTURE GOALS, MANIFESTING & VISUALISATIONS

"Whether you think you can, or you think you can't —
you're right."

— Henry Ford. Famously known for being the founder of the Ford Motor
Company, an American industrialist, business magnate and chief developer of
the assembly line technique of mass production

You've probably already had some thoughts about your future business and how that might look, feel and work. And, now that you have your limitless beliefs sorted, you're all set to go. But, until you know all the details of how you are going to achieve them, these thoughts can sometimes feel too big to achieve.

You might have tried manifesting and visualisations in the past but, I believe, there's one key point to start with if you really want to make these ideas work. Getting laser-focused on your big business goals and changing your mindset so that they are achievable is, to me, the key to real business success. That's where deciding on your 'Bigger Picture Goals' comes in.

BIGGER PICTURE GOALS

Bigger Picture Goals are those big chunky goals you want to achieve in your business. They might include writing a book, creating a podcast series or even launching your business. Here's a little exercise to help you decide on your Bigger Picture Goals to see what you will achieve.

HERE'S A FUN TASK I LIKE TO DO
AT THE END OF EACH YEAR

Imagine it's a year from now. Write yourself a summary of the amazing year you've just had! What were the big things you achieved in your business? What are you most proud of and what are you celebrating? How does it make you feel? Add a sentence or two about where you are and what you can feel, smell, taste and see around you. Remember, you can't be a great entrepreneur without looking after yourself, so add any health and well-being goals you'd like to work towards in the following year.

You could use some extra paper if you need more space.

Exciting, isn't it? What a fantastic year you have had. There's something about writing it all down that makes it feel incredibly realistic, doesn't it? But, before we move on, I want you to re-read your summary. Are you 100% sure that these goals are BIG enough? Yep, that's right, BIG enough! I'm sure you instantly felt a bit uncomfortable by that sentence. Did you play it a little bit safe? Have another look at what you've written and see if you can boost them in any way. Don't hold back!

Next up, transform these words into five fabulous goals for your year ahead.

1

2

3

4

5

Now, here's the fun part. You've got your five 'Bigger Picture Goals' for the year ahead. Let's make sure they become even more achievable by adding some manifestation and visualisations around them.

I'm sure you aren't a stranger to the words 'manifestation' and 'visualisation'. They are both buzzwords that have gained insane popularity over the last few years and, I can't deny it, I am a big fan! They've genuinely helped me build both my design business and Milspo, and have helped me plan for the future and see exactly what's possible.

However, some of you might be struggling with the idea that you can simply 'magic up' your perfect life; after all, it doesn't sound particularly scientific. And you are right... or maybe it's that imposter syndrome kicking in. All I can say is that it's both helped me and worked for me – and actually, if it works, perhaps it is okay. Honestly, what have you got to lose? Read this chapter and make your own mind up. You never know, it might just work for you too.

BUT WHAT EXACTLY IS MANIFESTING AND HOW DOES VISUALISATION HELP IN BUSINESS?

As you've seen in the last few chapters, I am a terrible sufferer of the dreaded imposter syndrome and lack of belief in my own talents – yep, it's something that I am constantly working on and it drives me bonkers! That's why I see manifesting and visualisation as a tool to help counteract this. It's my way of helping me find 'proof' that I can do it and that I am worth it because I have seen that it is possible and the route I need to take to achieve my goals.

Manifestation is the idea of bringing something you want into existence through aspirational thought. It's very on-trend now but, did you know, it's been hanging around since the 19th century?!

This concept of manifesting your reality via thought (or the 'law of attraction' as it's also called) is about the unity of your mind, body and the universe.

As a self-help exercise, manifestation focuses your thoughts on the desired outcome through mindfulness, visualisation and meditation to bring it into reality. Essentially, the idea is that you will bring your personal or professional goals into existence through the power of your brain.

Now, at this point, you might very well scoff at what you've just read. But don't forget how easy it is to attract those negative thoughts as your limiting beliefs start to become an unfortunate reality. Perhaps it's not so strange to believe that the opposite is possible after all.

THE LAW OF ATTRACTION

The law of attraction is the phrase given to these thoughts (both positive and negative) and the effects that they can have on our reality. This belief is based on the idea that people and their thoughts are made of 'pure energy' and that good or bad energy can attract similar energies.

There are conflicting ideas on how much you should or could embrace this thinking and I would strongly recommend you do your own reading around the subject as there has been lots written around it – both supporting and against the theory. Vex King's book *Good Vibes, Good Life: How Self-Love Is the Key to Unlocking Your Greatness* is a brilliant read if you are interested in exploring how energies can affect you.

For me, I use the law of attraction slightly differently as a way to try to focus on the positives and attract goodness all whilst detracting from the negatives. I also use it as a way to re-focus my goals and my journey as it helps me to believe that it's all possible.

When I set my bigger picture goals each January, I genuinely believe they are possible and that, with time, they will come to fruition – not because I want to sit back and have them happen to me. I know it's going to take hard work but I use this method to attract positive thinking and help banish imposter syndrome. It's a way for me to constantly believe that all of these dreams are possible, which means that I find them achievable. I use my interpretation of the law of attraction, coupled with visualisations, to make my big dreams easy to accept as reality. That way, I am not scared of them and can work towards them every day without giving up because they may seem too impossible. It's a way of mapping my route in my mind and feeling that it's possible.

Think of it this way. If you were driving from London to Manchester, you wouldn't just jump in the car and blindly set off because you just believe that you'll get there. Instead, before you set off on your merry way, you would stop to think about what you might need for the journey, how long it might take, if you need to bring anything with you and what you were going to do when you got to Manchester – all of that before you even got going! For me, manifesting, visualisations and the law of attraction work as my planning and roadmap for my business.

VISUALISATIONS

The word visualisation is quite self-explanatory and, for the purposes of this chapter, it's the process of visualising your business goals in detail so that they feel more possible and ultimately achievable. It can be done as part of meditation or, how I like to do it, as part of my journaling or by using a dream jar.

The key to visualisation is to get precise with what you want and how you will achieve it. You might imagine your future one year, five years or ten years from this very moment. What does your day look like? How does it feel to have achieved your dream? Where are you? What can you hear, smell and taste? How did you make this possible?

You could use guided meditation to experience the answers to the above questions, allowing you to imagine your future. Or, you could journal your future day, with a specific date, writing as your future self and celebrating all that you have achieved, like in the previous exercise.

Or, alternatively, perhaps you like the idea of a dream jar. Put simply, this is where you write down each of your goals or dreams onto small pieces of paper, fold them up and pop them in a jar. Each day you pull out one of these pieces of paper to read, close your eyes and sit with your dream for a few minutes, imagining how it feels. These will be the bigger picture goals that you have already worked on. The reason for keeping them fresh in your mind is to remind you of exactly what you are doing and why.

Practising those visualisations can make a massive difference to your business. I use them all the time, for every part of my business, and even for difficult life choices.

I use them as both a way to get excited about what the future might be like as well as to test my goals to see if they really 'feel' good for me and my business. They also keep me on track so that I always know the reasons behind what I am working on and why.

I interviewed the amazing Suzy Olivier, founder of Mothers of Enterprise, for the podcast. She uses manifesting in all that she does and has a wonderful reason why:

"I have my routines and my systems that keep me on track, and I use them with my coaching clients.

I teach every single day how you need to visualise that the end goal, that ultimate lifestyle or achievement or accolade, whatever it is, you need to constantly take yourself through it as if it's happening to you and your mind. For me, I've got this amazing dream of building our perfect house near the beach, so I (mentally) walk around that house on a daily basis. It gives me that little push because it reminds me why I'm working so hard and what I can provide for my family one day.

Those visualisations have had a real impact on me. They've changed my business completely and I'm so much happier. It's a constant daily injection of inspiration for me just to keep pushing on and challenging myself to create better content so that I can support more mothers in business."

And Suzy applies her knowledge and these techniques to the clients she coaches.

"I've realised that their biggest problem wasn't a lack of business knowledge. The biggest problem was often their mindset. I knew there was no way, no matter how good their business is, how good their product or service is, if the person behind it – the foundation of the business – is wobbly, if they haven't got confidence in themselves and don't truly believe in what they're doing, they don't think they're capable of huge success, or they have quite a few limiting beliefs about money and about what they are worth, success is just not going to happen.

I think so many businesses fail in the first year because people go into it thinking that a business is kind of going to be like a job. You'll just go at it until it stops working. People often don't realise that business is really hard. Entrepreneurship, starting a business, running a business and growing the business is hard work. There are days when you're going to want to hide under your desk and cry like a baby. You need to have that tenacity and that drive, and you have to know your deep why as to why you're doing it because, otherwise, you're going to fail.

I don't want to see a woman sacrificing so much of their time and energy into building something that will almost inevitably end up not succeeding. That's when I realised that the mindset issue had to be addressed."

And that really is the key to it all, however you choose to digest and reinterpret the tools in this chapter. If you don't believe it's possible, you will fail. That's because, when the going gets tough, those without that roadmap, without the tools we've discussed here on whatever level, will ultimately give up. But, if you believe it's possible that you can achieve these difficult things, then you are even more likely to succeed.

In the next chapter, we will look at some of my podcast guests who have found their way when life got hard, especially when this unpredictable Armed Forces life inevitably threw a spanner in the works. Perhaps, now you have read about manifesting, the law of attraction and visualisations, you will be able to see how their mindset got them through those tough times.

But, before we move on, I want you to take all that you have worked on in the last few chapters – your limitless beliefs and your five bigger picture goals for your business – and turn them into affirmations. This can be as simple as writing them onto pieces of paper for your new dream jar or adding them to Post-its and sticking them to your bathroom mirror. Put them front and centre so that every day, in the same way that Suzy walks through her dream house, you are seeing them, repeating them and starting to believe them.

AFFIRMATIONS EXERCISE

Grab a pen, your laptop, some Post-its or whatever feels best, and write out your limitless beliefs from the last chapter.

They should be in the first person – for example...

I have the energy and passion I need to work on my business in order for it to become the success it and I deserve.

Add to that your five bigger picture goals but in a way that you have achieved them – for example, I have just launched my new business and I have finished my first piece of work/ sold my very first product.

Pop them wherever you will see them most often and be sure to say them out loud. Imagine yourself achieving and feeling those things. It might feel a little bit awkward at the start but soon they will be part of everyday life and, before you know it, you will be feeling those things for real. You can achieve this, you are worthy.

'This negative voice in my head isn't my truth.
I can do this and I will do this – just watch me go!'

12

THROUGH ADVERSITY TO THE STARS

"You may encounter many defeats,
but you must not be defeated. In fact, it may be necessary to
encounter the defeats so you can know who you are,
what you can rise from, how you can still come out of it."

– Maya Angelou. American memoirist,
popular poet and civil rights activist

Per Ardua ad Astra – oh, look at me throwing a bit of Latin into this book! Are you impressed? Don't worry... it probably won't happen again. *Per Ardua ad Astra* is the motto of the Royal Air Force. It quite literally means *'through adversity to the stars'* - something that rings true for me as well as in most military marriages and, actually, through most businesses.

I hate to break it to you, reader, but if you thought military life was tough, life as a business owner takes it one step further.

At some point in business, you will want to give all of it up! Believe me, I have been there.

WHEN I ALMOST DELETED MY BUSINESS

Have you ever experienced those grotty days – usually in the middle of winter, when it's been drizzling for what seems like an eternity – and nothing seems to be going right? It's grey outside and it's somehow grey inside, too. Well, I've had a few of those.

As you know, I have my own design business – Design Jessica. It started in my first posting – the posting where I was painfully lonely and knew no one. Sound familiar? If you've chosen to move with your partner's job, then it's highly likely you've had one of those types of postings, too.

I loved being a freelancer at first. I had lots of work keeping me busy and it was all really enjoyable. I was getting commissioned for the types of projects that I could really get my teeth stuck into, such as designing children's books – the wonderfully big chunky, enjoyable ones. You know the ones with beautiful graphics, activities and stickers... life was good. I felt valued and inspired; I had a reason to get going every day. I felt so lucky that my inbox was full and, as well as enjoying the work, I was also making money in the process.

But then, as time progressed, the work started to dry up. It turns out that when you are out of sight, you quickly fall out of mind. The commissioning editors who would regularly send me work either got promoted, so the work they would commission out moved to someone new who didn't know me, or sadly they just forgot me! So I was left with very little meaningful design work and most of what I did get commissioned did nothing to make me feel much better.

It was winter, my husband was deployed and I was painfully lonely. I decided that enough was enough. I was giving it all up. I was going to close my website, delete my social media accounts and stop running my business. I was done. Instead, I was ready to become that 'normal housewife' that my mind had invented.

If only I had a 'real' job with a 'real' company. That would solve these problems, wouldn't it?

So, off I popped to see the welfare team at my then-local RAF base to ask for help in finding local employment. Their reply... *"Have you thought about volunteering at the local cats and dogs' shelter?"*

Now, before you turn your back on this book for incorrectly thinking that its author hates animals, I absolutely love this planet's four-legged furry friends – I had a few at home to look after already.* Unfortunately, life at a remote(ish) RAF base often means that there is very little in the way of meaningful employment. And, based on my visit, I knew in my heart that I wouldn't be getting any decent employment in the local area – the well-meaning welfare officer spelt out as much in plain black and white, and it was all because of the choices we had made as a couple to move with the serving partner's job. Basically, the long and the short of it was, there wasn't any work.

Update: now, I must stress that things have changed remarkably since this time. Thanks to the hard work of Heledd, from Recruit for Spouses, paving the way for the MOD to take notice of our employment needs and now the volunteer work of the Partner Employment Steering Group, which I am a proud member of, we are making fundamental changes to how the MOD and greater public view the military partner, spouse or other-half in terms of meaningful work – but it still can't go unsaid that this wasn't always the way. And, in this situation, I didn't have a chance of finding work – meaningful or not.

I guess that meant I didn't really have a choice. I didn't want to move *'home'* for my work, leaving my husband at his base and only seeing each other at weekends. So, my options were that I could either give up, be left wondering *'what if'* and struggle to find some traditional, local employment, or I could actually start turning things around, get stuck into this business and really make something from this unique (but not completely uncommon) situation.

Because you see, that's the key to it, really. Business life is going to be hard. Military life is undoubtedly going to be hard. But one day, you will realise that you have already hit the bottom, so the only way is up.**

And that's what happened. I accepted my reality and went on a mission to change it, aiming to make it the best it could possibly be. I picked myself up, dusted myself off and refocused. I fundamentally restarted my business from the ground up. I took time off from my designing to get my head around what I actually wanted to do and I rebuilt it from that point. I realised that I had fallen into the trap of accepting any design work that came my way at any price, leaving me feeling unvalued and uninspired.

Somewhere along the way, I had forgotten that it was my business and that I get to decide how it was run. I could determine when I designed, who I designed for, what I charged and, most importantly, decide what work I did.

This may all seem very simple on paper but, in actual fact, it takes some doing in real life. It takes hard work, determination and an awful lot of focus. But do you want to know a secret? I wouldn't change it for the world. My little business has taken me to some fantastic places and has given me the opportunity to enjoy some unique experiences. It's allowed me to work with clients worldwide, to contribute to my household financially and it even led me to make a keynote speech at the House of Lords!

That moment of clarity, the one where I really had reached the bottom, ultimately gave me the moment that we all need... that 'sliding doors' moment. Once we've experienced that moment, we realise that we can do amazing things when we have nowhere to go but up. In this case, it was restructuring and realising that business could be done another way.

It almost feels like military life is set to make us have these types of sliding doors moments at some point. And, unfortunately, it happens to the best of us. Let me tell you about my friend, Grace.

Grace is the founder of The Rainbow Tree, an artist and a children's author. Trained in the London art world, she worked for an international art consultant and Bonhams auction house. However, the day after she married her serving RAF husband, he was posted to a remote part of Scotland – a place where she couldn't find work in her area of expertise. After a year of looking, she began to stop following the art market or reading anything to do with the art world because it was just too painful and was doing nothing for her mental health. To add to this, her husband was deployed to Afghanistan for seven months and, as if that couldn't seem challenging enough, they found out the day before he left that she was pregnant.

"My background is in art history – I studied it at university. I knew early on that I wanted to start working in auction houses so, after university, I did a master's in London at Sotheby's Institute of Art. And they teach you everything. Not just about paintings but anything that auction houses sell such as furniture, ceramics and sculpture, and they set you up to work in the art world and auction houses. So I started working for Bonhams auction house and I LOVED it.

Then we got married. I thought I would be fine at the time because my husband had just graduated. I believed he would be posted in London and it would all be okay. But then he wasn't posted to London. We were headed to Scotland instead. I decided to quit my job and move with him.

I just couldn't find anything in Scotland within my field. It was a very tricky time for me, for my own personal development. Everything I had identified with myself, my personality and my work in auction houses started unravelling. It got to the point where I didn't really know who I was anymore. I actually had to stop applying for art jobs. I had to stop reading about it for a while because it just wasn't great for my mental state.

That first posting was so difficult and I definitely lost my way. My esteem just plummeted; I mean, really plummeted. I really got anxious about going to social occasions. I used to fear chit-chat and getting asked the question: 'What do you do?' It was not until I had my daughter two years later that I started slowly pulling myself off the ground, gathering bits of my identity back and trying to form a career that I could take anywhere we were posted.

I eventually got a job in a local charity shop to keep myself busy and then we found out that my husband was being deployed for seven months. So, I thought, I've really got to keep myself busy, especially when we then found out that I was pregnant a day before he left. I decided to do a teaching assistant course at a local school and, whilst there, everything sort of fell into place.

It was there that the spark reignited. I realised that art in schools was really in dire need. The primary school I worked at ran an art lesson for one hour every two weeks, which I thought was shocking. Since completing my master's, I had known that I wanted to write an art book but hadn't really known at what point that would ever happen... if it was ever going to happen. But I really felt that there was an opening in the market during my time there so I did some research into writing cross-curricular books, not necessarily to be used in schools but for parents and aimed at primary school kids."

Grace was able to reassess her situation, see that she wasn't happy and turn it into an opportunity that she would never have experienced if it hadn't been for her military life. But, as she goes on to say, there's one thing that really stops her in her tracks and that's when she's met with that annoying saying: *'You knew what you were letting yourself in for.'*

"I think it's really dangerous to say that – especially when you're in that mental state. It's very easy to start becoming bitter, especially with your serving spouse. You married them for a reason, right? You wouldn't have married them if you didn't love them but the worst thing a civilian person could say is: 'Oh, but you knew what you were getting into.' That's like saying: 'Oh, you're a marathon runner but, you know, you knew that your hips would probably give out eventually.' It's so unhelpful!

When you're yearning for something, if you feel like you have something else to give, then it's really important to make something of that because, otherwise, it will become a big elephant in the room with your spouse. They're doing what they love so, as spouses, we need to find a balance and have a medium to take with us if we are lucky enough to create our own business.

I knew that the arts were my passion and that's the area I'm meant to work in. And, equally, I think everything happens for a reason.

Even if it's just to help one person, one spouse in the military, I feel like I went through all of that to be able to say, I've been there too but look, we can create something for ourselves. So think about what you could do. Can you utilise that and take that with you on every posting you go to because you know you're worth it, you are clever and you have a lot to give."

Suzy Olivier, also faced adversity due to living the military life. However, with that said, she actually met and married her husband before he joined the RAF.

"My lovely husband and I ran a personal training and therapy company in Oxfordshire. I was a personal trainer and a corrective

exercise specialist, and we had a good company covering all of Oxfordshire and a great team.

Then, before I knew it, my husband ended up at Cranwell doing officer training. I was a South African Air Force kid growing up and I'm a pilot's daughter, so I never had any plans to become an air force wife.

He came home after officer training and then we went to Portsmouth. That's when I realised that my life, as I knew it, had ended. All that ambition I had to build a personal training career wouldn't work with all of these moves. Restarting a service-based business every two years or less just wouldn't work. In some cases, I think our shortest posting was 15 months. It's just not feasible.

Then, as we had kids on the way, I needed something that was moving-friendly, that could go all over the country and potentially the world with us.

I do think as military spouses, there's a very negative connotation attached to who we are as "dependents". I'm very much a glass-half-full kind of girl. I'm annoyingly optimistic and I'm always looking for the best in a situation. So when I realised that this military spouse life was my new life, it opened me up to opportunities and ways of thinking that I would never have entertained had we continued with our lives in the civilian, non-military world.

Now I want to use my experience of my last eight years as a military wife to inspire other military spouses. It's been the most successful eight years of my life and I'd say this opened me up to opportunities that have completely changed the trajectory of my life in the best way possible."

Mothers of Enterprise is a huge success! Suzy is now running her coaching business no matter where the RAF sends her and her husband. She has built that accomplished, sustainable business and has seen tremendous success as a result. But, I wonder if Mothers of Enterprise – a company that evidently makes her so happy – would have ever been born without the adversity she was faced with when trying to move her personal training company? Now, looking at how many mothers and military spouses she helps, there's no doubt that all of them would have missed out if she wasn't experiencing this unpredictable military life.

Another of my guests on the podcast, who has found and flourished thanks to the adversity encountered in Armed Forces life, is Eleanor Tweddell. Eleanor has made her mark as an author, with her book, *Why Losing Your Job Could be the Best Thing That Ever Happened to You*, and as a business owner of Another Door.

"The book was something I wrote when I lost my corporate job about five years ago. I was working for Vodafone at the time. I'd had a 23-year career in corporate doing all sorts of things, working for all kinds of amazing brands, but I was made redundant and thought, okay, this is my moment to change. This was a moment for me to do something completely different.

The only trouble was, I had no idea where to start and I was utterly lost. But, as these things do, they sort of aligned when my husband was just about to move on to a different location from where we were. That's when I thought: 'It's time to be self-employed and take my business with me' rather than me trying to fit around businesses every time we move."

Eleanor focused on finding the opportunities that came when one door closed. Finding her way after she was made redundant paired with the reality that military life no longer suited her career route meant that Eleanor's experience and life situation is now helping her clients find their own route.

Military Coworking Network founder Sarah Stone went from working at Number 10 to a new life in Germany almost overnight.

"In 2012, I worked in Downing Street for David Cameron. It was my dream job and I'd worked really hard to get in. Then my husband came home and told me that he was going to be posted to Germany. I really struggled for those two years in Germany and it was quite a dark period in my life.

When we moved back to Scotland, I got some contract work but, when that finished, I didn't know what to do. And that was how I started my business journey.

But that whole three or four-year period was really difficult for me. I was surprised by that because I've always been quite resilient but I found myself crying a lot, drinking a lot of wine and just not feeling very happy, and I hated him for it. What was more shocking was I really, really hated the military. I was so angry.

I joined the Army myself when I was 18 and I often say that that experience has made me who I am now. I wouldn't be where I am now – I wouldn't have worked for David Cameron if I hadn't had my military training, so I feel like I owe a lot to the military and I have a lot to be thankful to them for.

That's why I couldn't believe that I suddenly hated the military. I just thought this was wrong. It's not me and it's not them, it's just the situation, but there has to be something we can do to change it. It just didn't seem to make sense.

John, my husband, loves his job. If you cut him in half, army green runs through the middle of him – he just loves it, and I love him. I could have said to him: 'I'm miserable, please leave', and he possibly might. But it wouldn't make him happy. It would just be transferring one person's misery onto another. So I just thought, is there another way? Can we try and find another way?

I was trying to think what would have helped me as I couldn't do anything about the fact that he'd been posted to Germany. I couldn't do anything about the fact that I'd had to leave a job I loved but I could do something about the fact that I couldn't find work I loved.

So I started my business. I was coming out of my dark place and trying to think, how can I turn this into something positive? And how can I stop other people from going through what I've just been through because it was pretty unpleasant? And if it's been that unpleasant for me, someone who has experience working for the prime minister on their CV, it must be tough if you didn't have the chance to build a career before this happened to you.

I was trying to think of what we would need. I ran a social enterprise, doing public affairs for communities and grassroots campaigners. I was working with some communities involved with a Scottish government programme about taking over abandoned buildings and turning them into places where anybody could do anything – co-working spaces, craft workshops, cafes, nurseries etc. All kinds of things. The idea is that if you've got a beautiful building in your town and you don't want to see it turned into flats, you could turn it into an economically productive space. That's when I said to them that this is awesome and if they knew that military bases could do with one of these because there are often plenty of empty and available buildings on the base.

The guy in charge of the programme wanted to know more and asked if I would like to come to do a presentation to the Scottish Government's Veterans Minister on how it could help the military community. They loved it, saying everyone should have one... and then there was this pause. I just realised that it wouldn't happen unless someone made it happen. So that's sort of where it started."

The Military Coworking Network is now working in partnership with the MOD and Families Federations to run a pilot programme in the UK and Cyprus. It currently has nine coworking hubs and over 1,000 members and the model is being copied in US and Australian military bases. But, what strikes me the most is that without those uncomfortable years of struggle, the idea of the network would never have come to fruition. The same can be said for Grace, Suzy, Eleanor and me, too. The changes that came when military life knocked the stuffing out of us led to a rebuild that made us stronger than ever and gave us a real purpose – it revealed our 'why'.

Entrepreneurship, when faced with the ups and downs of the uncertainty of Armed Forces life, is not easy and it's far from pretty. I really hope that you've dodged the lowest points that sometimes come from this unsettled life and that you haven't reached that point. Or, maybe, you are currently living through something that has been thrown at you and has derailed you: a health worry, grief or the aftermath of the pandemic. Just believe that there is an end to it and you can find your way through this adversity. But remember... you were not put on this planet to take the easy road so, hold on tight, embrace the bumps and make sure you celebrate when you hit the stars!

In the next chapter, we will explore the 'why' behind your business and why it's essential to find out what will keep you on track when you hit any kind of adversity.

---

* And still do! If you follow any of the Milspo social media accounts or join any of our regular virtual meetups, you might be able to spot them every now and again.

** And if you read that WITHOUT having the tune of Yazz's '80s classic in your head, take five minutes to grab yourself a cuppa and get your boogie on. You're welcome!

13

FINDING YOUR WHY

"It's good to have money and the things money can buy.
But it's good, too, to check up once in a while and make sure
that you haven't lost the things money can't buy."

– George Lorimer, Journalist

The most successful businesses have a defined *why*. Having a *why* at the heart of your business gives you that reason to get started, keep going and make it into the success you deserve. Finding and focusing on your *why* can keep you on track when the going gets tough – you know, on that drizzly day around mid-January when you're swearing under your breath at the HMRC chatbot? That's precisely when you're going to need it.

And, when I talk about your *why*, I don't simply mean making a profit or gaining exposure. Instead, think of your *why* as your purpose, your belief or your cause. The thing that is the heart of your business and the reason why you keep building it.

I know you've probably already read about my *why* and the reasons behind how I got there in earlier chapters. But, for me, my *why* is that I want my community to flourish because that will make it easier for all of us to achieve what we want – and, if we achieve what we want, it means that we'll all be that little bit happier and, by default, I will be, too.

However, I have also seen the very dark side of life when things aren't happy and dreams aren't supported, and I don't want to see that happen to anyone else. And, closer to home, I want my baby boy to see me as someone who made a difference in this world in the way that she knew best. I hope that it inspires him to do the same.

For others, it can be something else that fuels their *why*.

I remember attending a talk by Julie Deane from The Cambridge Satchel Company. For those of you who are unfamiliar with her story, back in 2007, her eight-year-old daughter was being bullied at school. Julie knew that she needed to protect her daughter and have her enrolled in a new school as soon as possible. So, in order to cover the cost of the tuition fees, Julie decided that the best thing to do was start her own business. Sat at her kitchen table, with only £600 start-up cash, Julie created The Cambridge Satchel Company, which is now a key player within the fashion industry.

But Julie's *why* was and still is the reason behind her success. To begin with, she needed to take her £600 savings and generate over £24,000 a year... twice! After all, she couldn't put one child through private school and not do the same for her son.

> *"Isn't that what makes it exciting, a mission that drives you with such passion that there is no option than to succeed?"*
>
> *– Julie Deane. Founder of The Cambridge Satchel Company.*

Her company now supplies accessories to more than 120 countries and has received approximately $21 million in investments. It's been reported that Diane Kruger and Zooey Deschanel are supporters of the satchels, and it's not surprising considering that The Cambridge Satchel Company has collaborated with designers such as Comme des Garçons and Vivienne Westwood. And to think, it all started from that £600 in her kitchen. Julie discovered her *why* early on and that's why she felt that she could keep going, even when it got tough.

At the end of the talk, there was a Q&A. Up shot my hand with one of my favourite podcast questions:

"Julie, times are tough. I have a new baby, a husband in the military and the economy is in crisis – it's getting harder and harder to do business. How did you cope when you felt like giving up?"

Julie's simple but brilliant answer was that she couldn't give up. She needed her children to go to a new school, which meant that she needed to make enough to cover the school fees and having that very realisation meant that her business had to succeed.

She also added that her children were even more of an inspiration when building her business. They would help her in the stock room, sit together at the table doing their homework and accounts, and just help in any way those little hands could. Having her children so close to her business helped keep Julie's *why* at the forefront of her business focus, propelling her to succeed.

Even with all of the backing in the world – the money, the support, the training – if your heart isn't in it, starting a business will be a long, hard slog if you don't wake up every morning knowing what your *why* is.

So, let's hunt out your *why*.

It's time to be brutally honest with yourself in order to find your *why* – it can be your purpose, your cause, the reason you get up each morning. It means way more than having a successful business; it's the exact reason why you are building a successful business.

Start by answering the following questions:

1. **Why** does your business exist?

2. Is there a **specific cause** your business is supporting?

3. What do you **believe in,** both personally and professionally?

4. What do you want your business to **be known for?** What legacy would you like the business to leave?

And now, really drill into the answers to those questions and use the space below to work out anything that doesn't feel genuine. Have you focused too much on the outcomes or results and not your reason why?

Remember Julie? She needed her business to be a success so that her child could stop being bullied at school – that was her *why*. It wasn't about making a certain amount of money just because she wanted money.

SO, HAVE YOU TRULY FOUND YOUR WHY?

Write it here in all its glory. This is something you will be referring back to again and again – when the going gets tough, when you want to make big scary plans for your business or when you just need that little push to keep going, THIS will be your go-to reminder that will help you refocus and calm any uneasy feelings you may be experiencing.

However, your *why* can also be adapted and used directly within your business as its greatest marketing asset.

In 2010, British-born American author Simon Sinek presented The Golden Circle model in his now-viral TED Talk (it's had more than 66 million views and, if you haven't watched it yet, you should do that straight away! Like, right now. Seriously, pop off and take a look. I won't mind. I'll still be here when you're finished). He's split the structure of how a business or organisation should view itself into three levels, with the *why* being at the centre of The Golden Circle.

"The goal is not to do business with everybody who needs what you have. The goal is to do business with people who believe what you believe."

– Simon Sinek. American author and inspirational speaker

Every business owner or company knows **what** they do and the majority will understand **how** they do it, too. That's their assumed selling point – they make great burgers, nice bath salts, create lovely branding or beautiful computers – and then they tell you that you should buy some of what they're offering. That's what most people focus on when they are running their business. They tend to stop at the **how** and the **what**. Not very inspirational, is it?

The common thing you'll find is that organisations rarely know *why* they do what they do. And the answer to this isn't just to make money or have an incredibly high number of followers on social media – it's much deeper than that.

For Simon, *why* means: *What's your purpose? What's your cause? What's your belief? Why does your organisation exist? Why do you get out of bed in the morning? And why should anyone care?*

Having a purpose in business takes you one step ahead of the rest. It gives your business heart and attracts your greatest assets – the clients and customers who get you, are perfect for you and, in time, buy from you.

In his TED Talk, Simon uses Apple as an example. Apple is different to other technology companies in that they don't just sell a product. They sell a feeling. They sell a lifestyle choice. They sell to disrupters wanting to make a change. Their products are beautiful, easy to use and a designer's dream!* And, I'll admit, I have fallen hook, line and sinker for the Apple dream. You can't move around our house without a little glowing Apple icon flashing at you – much to my husband's and Alexa's disgust. He has yet to fall under the spell of the Apple! But, that's because he's not the audience they are aiming for. You don't have to sell to everyone.

> *"People don't buy what you do or how you do it,*
> *they buy why you do it."*
>
> – *Simon Sinek*

Apple sells its *why* to its customers front and centre (here's an epic lifestyle that we want you to have and it can all be yours with this lovely computer); meanwhile, their competitors are selling you their quality products but have failed to acknowledge the *why* (buy this lovely computer – we've spent years making it function really well inside).

Even if, just like my husband, you find more appeal in the tech part rather than the aspirational living element, you might think that Apple's hardware isn't as good as other companies. But that doesn't stop you from looking at other Apple products.

However, because Apple sells its *why* and that aspirational lifestyle feeling I mentioned before, it's even easier for them to sell their phones, tablets and online TV streaming. You might love your PC but have you ever really wanted to stream a channel from Microsoft or buy a mobile phone from Dell? Of course not, they are computer companies, but so is Apple. The huge difference between them all is Apple's strong focus on its *why*.

"If you talk about what you believe,
you will attract those who believe what you believe."

– Simon Sinek

So yeah, you'll need the epic product or service to back up your *why*, but no doubt you have that already – or why else would you still be reading this book? Like Simon, I believe that your *why*, when centred in the heart of your business and when projected from the inside out, can really set you apart as an entrepreneur. Not only will it help you keep going, but it will attract others who think the same way you do and who will also want you to succeed – and there can't be any greater starting point for a business than that!

* Believe me – I am one!

14

FAIL FORWARD AND FAIL QUICKLY

"Success is not final; failure is not fatal.
It is the courage to continue that counts."

– Winston Churchill. Prime Minister of Great Britain during World War II

The longer I have been in business, the longer I realise that some of the best entrepreneurs I know have made some of the biggest mistakes, yet they remain successful. Do you know why? Because, although they may fail massively, they fail well – and, most importantly, they fail forward and fail quickly.

But failing, especially in business, can be really frightening. I mean, frightening to the point where we no longer act. This chapter explores failure in business and how embracing those failures and reframing them as *'feedback'* – a wonderful opportunity to learn – can propel your outlook and business to the next level.

WHY ARE WE TOO FRIGHTENED TO FAIL?

It all harps back to our prehistoric survival brains. Remember how we talked about the sympathetic branch of the autonomic nervous system that saves us from tigers? It's the same part of the brain that kicks in here, too. Our subconscious brain jumps in and prevents us from doing anything uncomfortable that might reveal any potential weaknesses – the thing that attracts predators. It's basically your brain trying to keep you safe.

It also concerns how our parent's generation raised many of us. They were trained that happiness and success go hand in hand. So firstly, you need to do well at school, then well in your career, your marriage, and the list goes on – there's just no space for us to fail. This means we've convinced ourselves the best way to succeed is not to fail but how can you go through life not failing? By avoiding anything that isn't safe. We have taught ourselves not to be brave. If we don't take chances, if we don't step out of that safe and frankly boring comfort zone, we won't fail – but sadly, that also means that we'll just bimble comfortably along, staying the same and missing out on all of those amazing, potential opportunities.

This is why it always strikes me as bizarre that we, as entrepreneurs in the military community, feel this fear of failure most acutely. For a community that takes so many considered risks and continually accepts that our serving partners are expected to be brave in dangerous situations, we find it incredibly hard to take our own risks. Believe me! I know that feeling too well.

And this is really damaging when it comes to business. Playing safe and bumbling through life limits our ability and opportunity to create the businesses we deserve. Do you know what that ultimately leads to? **Regret.**

"Everything you've ever dreamed of is the other side of fear."
– George Washington Adair. Real-estate developer in post-Civil War Atlanta

Perhaps it's time that we embrace the idea of failure, start to feel uncomfortable and take those steps to try something; possibly fail in the process but, when we do, we fail forward. Remember that we are braver than we think.

WHAT DO I MEAN BY 'FAILING FORWARD'?

To ensure our big and small failures lead to a positive result and aren't just us repeating them, we must fail more intelligently – I like to call it failing forward.

Failing forward is all about making mistakes and then learning valuable lessons from them, which can then be applied going forwards. It's about creating and taking definitive action based on previous experience. It sounds simple but rarely do we manage it. In fact, we almost feel embarrassed by our failures, which means that we are inevitably doomed to repeat them – something that can spell disaster in business.

"Sometimes you win, and sometimes you learn."

– Robert T. Kiyosaki. Author of Rich Dad, Poor Dad

Mistakes! The thought of them can just make you cringe, especially if it happens in a part of your business that costs you money.

Here's my HUGE MISTAKE. It still makes me cringe to this very day and I can't quite believe that I am sharing it with you!

As you know, I used to design books. I was tasked with creating a series of five new books for the German market. When you're an English-speaking company, you outsource the translation of books to native speakers who will re-write the copy into the language you need – in this case, German. Once you receive the files from the translator, you simply copy and paste the text. The translators, editors and bosses also recheck it just to ensure that you have copied the right bits into the correct sections... so what could possibly go wrong?

On the first page of these five books, we added 'This Book Belongs To' as a lovely little personalisation for children to add their names. How lovely, or so I thought!

The German translator sent back the translation for the phrase 'This Book Belongs To' and I typed it into each introduction page... incorrectly.

This resulted in £25,000 worth of children's books being taken off the shelves and pulped! To put that into perspective, my entire year's salary as a junior designer was less than that. Can you believe it? It still makes me feel woozy to this day but, there's no denying, it was entirely my fault. Still, equally, that's why measures are put in place so that you don't just send the files that the junior designer has created to print without getting them signed off by (in my case) at least three bosses. With great power comes great responsibility* (and a pay cheque to match!), but, with no power and not much experience (and less pay, mind), comes these mistakes.

But what a lesson to learn as a junior designer and thank goodness for me that it was on someone else's time and budget.

Now, within my business, not only do I get a proofreader to check my work but I make sure to add a clause in my contracts to say that the client also needs to check their work, too – I have also avoided doing anything in German as a result of the slight mishap! So again, it's not about placing blame – it's about putting elements in place to protect yourself and ensure that it never happens again. The failure that I laid bare to you all just moments ago, turned into a lesson that I have never forgotten. It didn't halt me in my tracks. Yes, it was very uncomfortable but, ultimately, I will never make that mistake again.

THERE IS NO FAILURE, ONLY FEEDBACK

There is a series of online courses and workshops developed

specifically for Armed Forces Families, called The Warrior Programme, which enables individuals to manage their emotions and build resilience, focus and motivation as a way to help them succeed. I was lucky enough to take the course during the first lockdown in England back in 2020 and have found it truly life-changing. The course also focuses on providing tools to help its participants live a better day-to-day life and they touch on failure in one of their modules.

On The Warrior Programme, they say that *'there is no failure, only feedback'* – we are all expected to do things wrong from time to time but the feedback and how you adapt to those failures is what's most important.

This feedback could give you a new perspective on what has just happened. It can help you learn lessons ahead of the next time you attempt it. But, failing forward doesn't necessarily always need to be about something you gain. Sometimes, it can be a great way to learn what to get rid of.

Maybe it's a product or process that just doesn't work in your business. Perhaps you've launched a new product that isn't selling very well – no problem – it's time to cut your losses and move on but, most importantly, take the learnings with you in your business. You might even find that you have a more emotional response to a particular learning following a mistake. You might realise that you want to let go of anger or you may be able to shake off your lack of confidence. It doesn't always have to be about changing something – it can just be about letting go.

The next time you think you have failed at something, I want you to come back to these questions:

- What is there to learn from that experience?

- **What is it that needs to change next time to get the outcome you want?**

When you take back control, you're able to move forward faster and feel more confident in doing so.

R E M E M B E R . . .

The secret to failing well and failing forward is to learn from it. Treat every failure as a space to learn. Yes, it can be embarrassing, painful and maybe an expensive mistake, but it's also the best way to learn.

F A I L   =   F I R S T   A T T E M P T   I N   L E A R N I N G

Have an honest look at where you went wrong, why you think it's a failure and how you can progress when you do it again next time. What are you learning from this?

**B U T   W H A T   I F   Y O U   A R E   T O O   W O R R I E D   A B O U T   F A I L U R E
T O   E V E N   G E T   S T A R T E D ?**

There's a chance that the fear of failure might even be enough to stop you in your tracks. Especially when you want to start a business or make a big business decision, it can feel uncomfortable or even too worrying. And, sometimes, you might find valid reasons not to take the first step towards those goals. So, it's time to ask yourself whether there's a genuine risk or whether you might be creating limiting beliefs that stop you from receiving what you deserve.

**H E R E ' S   A   L I T T L E   E X E R C I S E   T O   D O   I F   Y O U   A R E
T A K I N G   O N   A   N E W   P R O J E C T   O R   I D E A :**

When you find yourself at a crossroads in business, when there is a risk of failure, ask yourself: **"What's the worst that could ACTUALLY happen?"**. Now write it down. But, not just that one sentence, really get stuck in. Explore what could happen and the results that could come from your choice. Is this worst-case scenario actually likely to happen? Does this, in fact, come from a place of fear or worry about failure? What could actually happen if it all went well? And how can you get back on track if the worst-case scenario happens? What might you learn?

Now, stop and think, how does that feel? Is it okay – then what are you waiting for? Does it make you feel uncomfortable – are you, in fact, worried that you could become a success?

So, at this point in Section Two, you will have started to notice a shift in your perception of yourself and how you look at things, especially uncomfortable things around building your dream business. In the following few chapters, we will examine how others might perceive you and any other external factors that might limit your business potential. But, before we dive into that, I just want us to take a moment to remind you of our mantra from page 58.

"This negative voice in my head isn't my truth.
I can do this, and I will do this – just watch me go!"

Things might have started to feel a little bit more uncomfortable or real, or maybe you're really excited! Just remember, you can do this, and you will do this!

* To quote Peter Parker's, aka Spider-Man's, Uncle Ben!

15

MOURNING MY CAREER

"I attribute my success to this:
I never gave or took any excuse."

– *Florence Nightingale. British nurse, social reformer and statistician*

I often sit and think about a parallel universe. Have you heard the science about the fact that there may be millions of other parallel universes where precisely the same things are happening but with ever so slight differences? I sometimes wonder what I would be doing if I hadn't met my husband: where I would be and what I would be doing in that parallel universe – I think we all must do it every now and again. And, one thought that always pops up... what would I be doing for work?

As I mentioned before, I am primarily a graphic designer and, at the time I left my job to ultimately start my business as a freelancer, I was a middle-weight designer and mid-career, making decent money and working my way up the corporate ladder.

I sometimes get a little bit sad when I think of who I might have become if I had stayed on that path. I'm not ashamed to admit that it can be really difficult when you have a high-achieving partner not to be a teeny bit jealous of their success.

Take the medals, for example. The number of partners I have heard say they should get medals, too. For me, it's all about the career. I have always wanted to match my husband in what he's doing. Not because I'm competitive but because that's the woman I was when I met him. I was a career woman and it's felt like every single time we've been posted, I have had to start again. When he has come home from his new exciting job, I've been green with envy because, for me, life has always seemed to grind to a halt or worse, taken a step backwards each time we're posted. For him, I imagine a few things have changed but, ultimately, he's still working on his career and its progression.

For so many years, I have spent time mourning my lost career. I've felt it was whipped away from me whilst I was in my prime and, truth be told, I have never really gotten over it. It's hard work celebrating your partner's career when you don't have one to match. But that's where I went wrong. You see, I had convinced myself that I had lost my career when, in reality, it was just a new stage in my career because you never really lose anything – you just continuously grow and change.

LIFE IS ALWAYS ABOUT EXPERIENCES AND LEARNING

Over the years, as I interviewed my podcast guests, one thing started to become clear – as military partners, my guests had also had to adapt their view of traditional employment. At each point of change, it had been a little uncomfortable but the learnings and experiences gained because of that change ultimately led them to where they are today – at a new career stage.

Take lovely Georgie Muir, for example, who was working as a chiropractor until a posting to the USA meant that she had to adapt.

"I loved being a chiropractor – I had lovely practices and lovely patients. But, with military moves every couple of years at most, rebuilding the business meant too much blood, sweat and tears. There came a point where my husband received a posting to the US – which was a joint decision – but, once we looked deeper into it, we realised I couldn't practice because of the industry I was in. So it left me completely stumped and essentially spiralling into this question of, well, if I'm not Dr Muir, Chiropractor, then who on earth am I? And what value do I even have?'

I think we have all been at the point where we have struggled to find our value in this ever-changing world, where others around us seem to have it sussed. So it's particularly obvious when our closest ally – aka our spouse, partner or other-half – appears to move into their next post almost seamlessly. For Georgie, that American posting gave her time to reassess and discover what was next for her. She picked up on something her dad used to say to her as a child:

"Although it wasn't necessarily the prettiest place to be digging into, doing the work to find my way back to 'me' was amazing. And that was all stimulated by this thing that my dad used to say to me which was: 'The world is your lobster.'

So it's not just about what you can do but what you want to do. What do you want to be? What do you want to create? That's when I thought, you know what, this is my opportunity to really work out what my lobsters are and set about chasing them down, really bring them into my reality.

I have this window of opportunity – I can either crumble under it or I can find my way to really thrive within it and connect with what I need, connect with what I want and make it happen. And so I started blogging and named my blog Chasing Lobsters. And everything has grown from there."

And that's the key – do you crumble under the change or thrive at the prospect of opportunity?

Someone who's made a success of finding those opportunities is Eleanor Tweddell, who I mentioned in a previous chapter. She inspired others to take a breath between jobs, to mourn what once was but to also examine where they are and where they want to head next.

"So I think I learned the hard way that when you lose a job, or as we experience every time we move, we're almost resetting and going again. If we don't take that time just to reflect, take a breath and think 'Where am I at right now?', we just plough on through. But how will I know what I want from this unless I take that pause to think about it? What are the opportunities out there? What else could I be doing? We're probably not doing ourselves justice.

One of the things I realised when I lost my job was that I probably hadn't really thought about why I was doing what I was doing in the first place. Was I still thriving, was I still growing? I just got up and went to work and my work frequently came home with me, too. I was in quite a senior role so it wasn't in an environment where you've got a lot of learning and development. I didn't add that reflection time. So that is definitely one of the messages I have learnt so far – make time for that pause that appears between one door closing and the next one opening."

But it's a harsh reality to live through. Leaving full-time employment to pursue a business – and, like in my case, picking between a career and being a couple – can be tough. Eleanor found this out, too.

"I left Virgin Atlantic – flying around the world in first class working for Richard Branson – to join a military community. You know, we can mourn it. I think that's the first step. That's what I'd say anyway. I think sometimes we're very apologetic about it but, ultimately, I've chosen

it. That beautiful saying – 'you know, I knew what I was getting myself into' – that gets gifted to us now and again. You knew what you were signing up to? I think, actually, no, we didn't.

Nobody knows what they're signing up for in life. Yes, it's a choice to some small degree but, it's still okay to have those feelings. It's okay to look back at our lives and go, 'Oh, God, that was hard.' But also to do it in a way of celebration that you can then take forward and apply to similar situations in the future. And I think that's the key bit.

So when we've got a door closing, we often just close it and don't look behind it again. We just plough on or simply focus on the next door and shut out all those feelings. But, if you can embrace those feelings, then it's fine to look back at that door. It's fine to go: 'You know what? I was absolutely nailing it – I loved it there' and start actually remembering yourself in that space. You can bring all of those positive parts into where you're at now. I often think to myself: 'Are there elements I can still do and enjoy in my next step?' That's the first step for me. It's like not pushing it down and not spending that emotion – it's trying to celebrate it and go, okay, I'm still me; I'm still that person that had all that joy once upon a time."

But what if you feel that you are just too upset to take that first step to start mourning? In the podcast episode, Eleanor shared her thoughts on this very question:

"I think there are different levels; I believe there are other things that motivate people. No one knows what would have happened anyway because we all evolve. You probably wouldn't have been still in that job, that's just life. But one of the things we have to keep checking in with ourselves – going back to that point about creating space – is to reflect and ask yourself: 'Where am I at right now?' So you kind of go back but then bring yourself into the present.
This gives you the opportunity to take a look around you; take a look

at all the fantastic stuff you're doing. Look at all the opportunities that are coming your way. And, if you don't feel like that's where you're really at, what are you doing to create those opportunities? I see many people sitting in the wallowing space, which is fine for a little bit. But if you sit in the space of wallow – constantly thinking or telling yourself: 'This is a nightmare. This is so unfair' – if you spend too much time in that space, that will become YOUR space.

It's about trying to take that first step out and say, okay, not feeling great, but how do I just start changing the narrative of what I'm telling myself? How can I start flipping it to say, I'm doing alright, I've got an amazing husband/partner, life, I've got all of this stuff around me? I've got all of these opportunities. That person I was ages ago... I'm still that person. So what can I do with it now?

There are always choices. There are always opportunities but you have to put yourself out there and change that narrative, and every time you hear yourself thinking, 'This is hard; this is so unfair,' it doesn't mean you have to push it away and make positive plans all the time.

I describe it as catching it, holding it and just saying: 'I've heard you, but you're not taking over me today.' I'm not going to be this wallowing person. What can I do today? Get out there and do something. So I think there are elements of it's fine to wallow, but own it and capture it and change the narrative."

DOES THAT LIFE EVEN EXIST ANYMORE?

Here's the thing. There isn't an 'old' me and a 'new' me – there's just, well, 'me'. Even if there is one of these alternative universes, that isn't really going to make a massive difference to me – right here and now. I only know about and have the universe that I wrote this very book in!

Eleanor says: *"We give ourselves a story of what we think would have happened or where we believe we would have been and actually*

168

don't know any of it in the first place. You could have just become this huge person in your industry who got greedy and horrible. And you became this horrendous person that was amazingly successful and rich, but still a horrible person. Who knows what could have happened to any of us in the future? The point is, that was then and it was amazing, but this is where I'm at now; what will I do in the future? We all own our futures."

And we really, really do. You can find yourself living in your past or, perhaps, after a little bit of self-care and re-accepting a change as an opportunity, dive into your future and do amazing things. I have achieved so much since making the leap to self-employment. I would never have achieved mind-blowing things if I hadn't met my husband – I mean, look! You are reading a book that I've written. Not many of my old workmates could say that and 'old Jess' certainly couldn't either.

I previously spent too much time in my past and it was getting in the way of my fantastic future. I imagine many military partners feel the same way at the arrival of a new posting. Dragged away from their 'old life' without much choice. What if we could let that go and imagine our bright, brilliant future in which we could achieve absolutely anything we set our minds to?

That would be nice, wouldn't it?...

16

HOW YOUR PARTNER CAN BE YOUR BIGGEST BUSINESS CHEERLEADER!

"I have yet to hear a man ask for advice
on how to combine marriage and a career."

– Gloria Steinem. Journalist and social activist

Time to address the elephant in the room.

"What does your husband do?"

I can almost feel your eyes rolling from here!

It's probably the most dreaded question you could ever ask a military spouse. So, why is it that when we mention that our partners are in the military, everyone...

No .1 – assumes that they are male,

No .2 – that we are married, and

No .3 – thinks their job should become the next part of the conversation.

What about me and what I do?!

I have lost track of the times I have been asked this, long before anyone wants to know about me. It usually comes up in conversation

171

when someone is curious about why I have just moved to the area, or why we haven't met before, or most commonly where my husband is... "He's deployed" is the standard answer. It's just SO annoying!

I get it, it's interesting, but could we do me first? Sometimes people are just excited and intrigued about what he does. Whereas in other cases, sadly, some people are very standoffish about it, as they don't see the good bits of the Armed Forces, such as the humanitarian support and the innovation that the defence provides. There's just this assumption that it's all about invading countries and war. I remember a very odd conversation I had with someone about ten years ago in which she basically told me off for the Falklands War... despite the fact that I was a tiny baby when it took place. No matter what I tried, she just wouldn't let it go, as if I had a say in foreign policy back in the '80s.

Then there's the opposite side, where people seem to get too excited about it and spend a lot of time telling me about my own life *(Yes, you absolutely read that right!)*. I once had a very long and painful conversation with an MP (who quite frankly should have known better) telling me how difficult my life was as an "army wife" and how worrying it is to stay at home waiting for my husband to get back from war. I just wish he'd let me get a word in edgeways so that I could point out that my husband wasn't deployed (this time) – he was just the other side of the room and very much still in the RAF!

It must be something to do with popular culture but the great British public seem to have a weird fascination with the military, taking ownership of it along the way wherever they can.

This fascination is something that gets drawn out in my life quite often. Friends I've not seen in a while ask what he's up to before asking how I am. New acquaintances, who commonly ask me why I've just moved here, find themselves quizzing me about my husband's job. And to be fair to them, it is exciting and I am so very proud of what he's doing but, one day, I'd quite like someone to be fascinated by what I do.

Because, for the military partner, sometimes it can feel like our entire existence revolves around what our serving person does. After all, it's sometimes the reason behind where we live and where our children go to school. And, in my case, it's the whole reason I started my business so sometimes, just sometimes, I get really bloody bored talking about it.

When it comes to the wonderful Milspo Network, I also choose not to tell people about my husband – mostly because Milspo is not about him. Milspos values mean that the number one priority is to showcase businesses run by military spouses, partners and other-halves within and outside of the network. But also because, in the same way that I have zero influence over my husband's career, he should have little influence over what I do in my career. Now, before anyone starts, that doesn't mean that we don't support each other – it simply means that we are both big enough to do our own thing successfully without having the other one prop us up.

Although we might not feel the need to talk about our serving person's career all the time, that doesn't mean that their job doesn't of course affect our business. It is being married to the military that makes running a Milspo business so challenging after all. But you can turn that to your advantage. Since your serving person understands military life like the back of their hand, they are well aware of the challenges you face. That can make them a massive champion and ally for spouses, partners and other-halves in business.

In fact, having the support of your partner is incredibly important when it comes to starting your business. Nadine (owner of Forces Family Finance) and I spoke about the importance of having your serving person on board when running your own business.

WHY HAVING A SUPPORTIVE PARTNER IS THE ONLY WAY YOU CAN RUN YOUR BUSINESS

"I founded Forces Family Finance around six years ago. It was born from a combination of my professional background in financial services – namely in providing financial advice around mortgages and insurances – and my personal experiences of military life, because I've been married to a Royal Engineer for almost two decades.

So, for me, it just seemed perfect timing and something that I always wanted to do. I was getting fed up with trying to find a new job at each posting, which we all have to do, and I just had a real hunger to set up a business that combined all of that together to help people."

Nadine started her business with three tiny children but, despite this, has proven that starting a business with three mini cheerleaders is still absolutely possible.

"It was really hard. There wasn't a lot of sleep going on. There wasn't a lot of couple-time going on. There wasn't a lot of me-time going on. I think it's important to be really candid about that. You've got to be realistic – these things don't happen easily otherwise everyone would do it, but my husband and I agreed from the start: now's the time. It was always a dream of mine and something that he wanted to support me in. To a certain extent, you're going to be tired and lacking in you-time and couple-time anyway when you've got young children and babies.

So, we just went for it and the first few years were ridiculously hard. I feel like we've really come out the other end of it now and we're genuinely starting to see the fruits of our labour and it's such an amazing feeling. But you've got to stick at it. You have to be tenacious.

I think it is really, really important to have your partner or your family on board and for them to understand that this is the time and commitment that's going to be involved. And make sure that they're happy with that and maybe set yourself boundaries from the beginning. When I did my business plan and its goals, part of working out what my week and month looked like was making sure that I scheduled in family time and time with my husband. Because if I wasn't achieving that, I was losing at life, really."

During the podcast episode together, we went on to discuss just how important it is to receive support from the person you are closest to in your life, whether that be your husband, wife, spouse, life-partner, other-half, soulmate… or whichever words and terms you want to call them.

"I really strongly believe that their support is just so important and where I've mentored and helped people in the past, I have noticed a distinct difference between those who have that support and those who don't. So, I do feel really, really fortunate.

But I think it's having that conversation about your shared goals to help you both stay focused when things are a bit moody or you may end up feeling a little bit resentful or down.

For me, when I launched the business, we had a very clear, smart goal of how in a five-year period, we would get to the point where this business was creating an equivalent of a full-time income or it just wasn't going to work and I'd call it a day.

We were always very, very clear and driven on that. It's what we've held on to and, for us, that five-year goal was very specific as that was when my husband would reach his full military career and we'd be looking to transition. He hasn't signed off this year though because of Covid but that was the plan at the beginning and what we were aiming for and I think that shared goal and vested interest in making it successful is what kept us both going.

If you're not communicating those ideas, it can be really easy – particularly in the first few years where you're not really making that much money but you're crazy busy – for resentment to build. So, you've got to talk and have those shared ideas of what is the point of this?"

Just like Nadine, my husband has been an integral part of the planning for my business and it's been a really important part of building both Milspo and my design business, Design Jessica.

It's so important to have a proper conversation with your partner if you are considering starting your own business – not because you need their permission (it's not the 1940s!) but because this journey is going to be a damn lot easier if you have their support.

Some of the best business decisions I've made to date – including writing this book – get thrown past my husband because not only is he my biggest supporter but also because he knows more than anyone how Milspo works. After all, he's been there since the very beginning and I have also included him in the decision-making process along the way. He's also one of my biggest cheerleaders, which means that in a weird twist of fate, he spends just as much time talking about my career as I do talking about his.

TIME TO TELL YOUR PARTNER

First up: they aren't going to be as excited as you, which isn't a bad thing. It's YOUR baby and they are just here to support, so don't be downhearted if they don't look all that excited. This simple exercise is just a way to prepare you so that you aren't caught off-guard by their response, should it not quite be what you expect.

Here are my key talking points that you might want to consider before speaking to your partner. They are bound to ask you these questions, so it's good to have a rough idea of the answer – or not, if you haven't quite decided yet. If you don't have your partner with you right now or don't have one, maybe ask a close friend who can act like a sounding board for you.

1. **"What are you going to do?"** You should have a fair idea of what you might like to do now that you have completed Part One of this book. Pop your thoughts below.

2. **"What are you going to call it?"** A fiddly question at the best of times but they'll want to know all the same. Try to have an answer ready or perhaps ask your partner to be a part of the decision making – who doesn't love a good brainstorming session?

3. **"How much is it going to cost us?"** Not the easiest of topics to discuss but one of the super important ones. It's time to consider finances! Now, there's no need to get into the nitty-gritty of it all and go into lots of detail, but this is a question that very well may be asked since it will inevitably have an impact of some sort on the overall household.

4. **"How much time is it going to take?"** Ahh yes, time. Your partner may want to know the answer to this question out of curiosity as to how your life together, as you know it now, will change as a result of your new business.

As I mentioned above, this is absolutely NOT about asking your partner's permission to start up and run your own business. This is simply a method you can use to prepare yourself, as you embark on this very early and sensitive stage of your business, for any negativity you might get once you start telling the world about your new venture. You don't want to be knocked back before you've even started – then you would be really missing out and all because of someone else's inadequacies.

REMEMBER, THIS IS YOURS AND ONLY YOURS

You can do this and you *will* do this! Don't you worry about anyone else and especially don't worry about what they think of you as a military partner. Yes, they'll be intrigued by your partner's job – I don't think that's something that will ever change – but wait until they hear about you! And, if you have your serving person as your biggest cheerleader, then that's even better.

"If you think the UK Armed Forces are impressive,

you should see what their spouses,

partners and other-halves are achieving."

– Jess Sands. Founder of the Milspo Network

*"Everything you've
ever dreamed of is
the other side of fear."*

– *George Washington Adair.*
Real-estate developer in post-Civil War Atlanta

PART THREE

MY BEST TIPS

LEARN FROM THE MISTAKES AND SUCCESSES OF MY BUSINESS, AS WELL AS THOSE IN THE COMMUNITY

Welcome to part three! This section is all about real-life business – warts and all! The mistakes, disasters, crises, good days, wins, celebrations and huge successes.

We've worked on the technical bits and your mindset, and now I want to show you how putting it all into practice can help build that business you deserve.

However, there will inevitably be some bumps in the road along the way. Like all things worth the struggle, you will come across difficulties set to trip you up. You might find them early on – even getting started can be frightening – or later in your business journey, when bigger things are happening.

This section will give you real-life, on-the-ground success stories and examples to show you that you can do it, too. From my own experiences, alongside those of my pals – many of whom I have interviewed for the podcast – you'll hopefully finish this chapter with a heightened sense of motivation, enthusiasm and drive to succeed in your business.

It also features lots of practical advice about how to run a business through this unique military life, whether that be through postings, deployments or running a business with children in tow. As with the previous chapters, you might feel that not every one is relevant to your circumstances but I encourage you to read them anyway. Everyone has a nugget of goodness that might surprise you and therefore help you along your way.

17

HOW TO RUN A BUSINESS
THROUGH A MILITARY POSTING

"The pessimist sees difficulty in every opportunity.
The optimist sees the opportunity in every difficulty."

– Winston Churchill. Prime Minister of Great Britain during World War II

Now, it's pretty inevitable that when you are partnered with someone in the British Armed Forces, they will get posted at some time or another.

Military postings are where the serving person is moved into a new job or posted into a new role, both abroad or in the UK. Sometimes this can be in the same base as they are already stationed at but, the majority of the time, it can be to a different base in the UK or, potentially, anywhere in the world. Usually, they are accompanied postings, which means that you might choose to go, too. You will have access to military married quarter accommodation and a team of movers who will help you with as much or as little as you'd like. Now, I'm not going to go into the fine details of military moves as, quite frankly, there is a lot of MOD admin that might change and, also, it's a long and tedious process that you can only truly understand when it happens! Or when it all changes at the last minute.

But, with all that said, I really want to help you if you are moving and running your own business. Yes, it can be done!

That's why, in the following few pages, you'll find my best tips for surviving a military move when you own and run a small business. All of these tips are tried and tested within my own business, and I have even asked my best business pals to contribute their ideas, too. At the time I wrote this book, I had been married to my husband for almost ten years and we have just completed our seventh house move so, it's fairly safe to say, I have A LOT of experience in moving my business across the UK.

It has been intense and challenging, to say the least, but it's also given me some of the best times I have ever encountered. There's nothing like moving every ten minutes to help you see just how strong your marriage is and just how kind this military community can be.

Making your business transient is crucial if it's going to survive this crazy military life. We need a business that's accessible and open to clients and customers no matter where we find ourselves living or the time zone we find ourselves in.

As a business owner and wife of an RAF husband, I chose to relocate every couple of years as his job dictates, meaning that I take my design business, Design Jessica, with me.

Here are seven of my best tips to help you with a military posting as a business owner...

CRM SYSTEMS AND YOUR CUSTOMERS

I couldn't be without my CRM (customer relationship management) system. It allows me to keep my clients' details and work streams in one place and it's the first place I head to after my morning coffee. I use Pipedrive but others include Asana, which I have heard fantastic things about, and Basecamp, but there are loads out there. Most offer a month's free trial, which you can try out before signing up. It's a great way to keep in touch with clients you have made a good relationship with before moving home.

The most influential people in your business are your clients. It can be incredibly difficult to find new clients but much easier to look after your existing ones.

As soon as you know that you are moving, email your clients and explain the situation and how you intend to work with them in the future. You can do this through your email list should you have a product or business, or individually if you are a service-based business.

The secret here is to stay completely transparent so that your customers and clients know the situation and realise what's happening should you get busy and aren't replying to their emails in the same timeframe that you usually would.

LOST CLIENTS

One of the saddest parts about moving locations is that some of your clients will forget you. I try to counteract this by sending them the odd email or even a Christmas card each year but, usually, if you aren't around and reminding them of your existence, you sometimes get forgotten. I don't let this happen when it comes to my most important clients and will quite often travel quite a way to see them in person. I have also been known to send them flowers on their business birthdays, too. It's a great way to keep in touch and stay at the forefront of their minds.

SOCIAL MEDIA SCHEDULING

Keeping up with social media can be an absolute nightmare when you're in the middle of moving. When the internet isn't switched on for a couple of days or the router is somewhere beneath a pile of other boxes, the last thing you're thinking about is a Facebook post. My tip? Schedule ahead.

There are loads of apps to help you schedule posts for later on. I've used Hootsuite, Later and Meet Edgar, all with varied results. Some you have to pay for and some are free for a limited number of accounts. So have a nosey to see which one suits you and your business the best.

Facebook's scheduling tool, Meta Business Suite, is free to use and also posts to Instagram. It's even better for your analytics but it won't integrate any other platforms.

Can't think of anything to schedule? Share about your move! People like to see the human side of your business – however, be sure to keep security at the forefront of your mind and avoid geo-tags or any identifying details in your posts that could reveal where you are.

NETWORKING

I find the best way to find new clients and helpful local businesses once you arrive, is through networking.

There are hundreds of networking groups available and it does take a bit of trial and error to find the great ones, but it is 100% worth it.

I love my networking groups. Not only are they great at helping to find new clients but it's also lovely to talk business with like-minded people.

There's much talk about the military community connecting with other networking communities and there are loads out there, so go and test them out! If you are keen to build a network that you can take everywhere the military takes you, then check out the free Virtual Networking events we run in the Milspo community.

CHANGE YOUR ADDRESSES

There's no way around it – it's one of the most annoying things to do when you are moving but it's even more annoying if you forget to do it. Take some time to list your business profiles, subscriptions, insurances and deliveries so that you can plan the best dates to change them.

If you have a registered business address, you won't need to worry about this too much as it won't change, but you should let HMRC know about your contact address. You don't want to miss out on any important post.

You can also set up a redirection service with Royal Mail for at least six months after you move should you forget to update anything important.

GETTING PERMISSIONS

No matter where you are posted, you might need to ask permission to run your business from home, if that's your plan.

Read your renter's contract or, if you are in Service Family Accommodation (SFA), check with welfare at your new location to find out their suggestions for registering with whoever looks after your housing.

In my experience, it is always different on each base – sometimes, it's done via email and sometimes through your serving partner's chain of command but the best thing to do is ask. They may even have some valuable information about your new location whilst you are there.

TAKE TIME OFF

Finally, the most important one, which I found out the hard way! Being posted is tough and tiring. More tiring than I ever expected. I swear the boxes breed and multiply when you've got your back turned.

The most important tip I can give you if you're due to be posted, is to book some time off from your business. Yes, it might seem like you can't and posting dates will often change but, as long as you give your clients enough notice to send you work and have some systems in place for that time, you will be fine. They are human too and will understand.

Make sure you have an out-of-office on for your emails explaining that your internet access and work availability may be limited and email your most important clients personally, so they know you will be away for a bit. I always exaggerate how much time I will be away from the office just in case it all takes a bit longer than planned. Then, if it doesn't, they'll be happily surprised and impressed that I am back early.

There are no two ways about it – moving home with a business adds another level of stress and admin, but it is possible. I should know, I've done it a few times, so you can do it too! As long as you plan and rely on the systems mentioned above, it should all go as seamlessly as you can hope for. Of course, things will always spring up to challenge you but, after all that effort, you'll be able to restart as smoothly as possible. Plus, you'll be able to take advantage of all the new opportunities in your new location. How exciting is that!

In the next chapter, I'll discuss how it's possible to move further to an international posting. If you're due one, you can also use the tips in this chapter to help.

18

HOW TO RUN A BUSINESS THROUGH AN INTERNATIONAL MILITARY POSTING

"I can't change the direction of the wind,
but I can adjust my sails to always reach my destination."

– Jimmy Ray Dean. American country music singer,

television host, actor and entrepreneur

As yet, I've not had an international posting. We've moved a lot but only around the UK. However, as I said at the start of this book, if there's something in business that I haven't experienced for myself but think is relevant to business, military life or both, I will hunt out my best business experts and give you their expertise in place of mine.

Thankfully, our community is full of them and I have been lucky enough to interview a lot for the podcast series. For example, in 2020, just as we went into lockdown, I interviewed the incredibly inspiring Georgie Muir.

Georgie runs Chasing Lobsters – a coaching company for professional women working in leadership positions. She has had two international postings with her serving husband, one of which was why she launched her business. What follows is an excerpt taken from the podcast, when I spoke to Georgie about her moves and how she managed those overseas postings.

"Learn from my mistakes: give yourself a grace period and do not anticipate work continuing at the same pace without taking a break during the move. I did this on our return from Turkey; my husband deployed three weeks after we moved back and we weren't in our military quarter yet. And, within that, I thought it was a brilliant idea to keep working for as long as possible – it wasn't!

When running a business whilst moving internationally, you need to permit yourself to pause the business. That can feel scary for many people, especially if the business is new... I've been there. So that's why I thought I was going to power on through.

Then, after that pause, you realise that actually, we are still here – I can still pick up the pieces and crack on as initially expected. But obviously, there are things you can do to prep and prepare for that. If you are nervous, I would recommend that you acknowledge it and get into action to do the things that feel supportive to you, allowing you to be gentle with yourself during the move. Give yourself that little bit of comfort that, actually, I am willing to take this because I know that I've got A, B, C and D in place to support me during this time, and I've got other plans in place for when I revisit work afterwards. So, you're acknowledging that you're a little bit nervous but you're then getting into action and moving forwards."

And then the emotional strains of moving…

"Acknowledge the energy that it takes and the recovery that you're going to need. I think recognising that the emotional challenge of any move warrants respect is key.

So that would be recognising the magnitude of the event of any move – whether that's international or within the UK. It's something that we get a bit blasé about within the military world. It's like, 'Hey, we've done this before. I'm a pro at this and it doesn't matter.' It's still an enormous life shift, a massive logistical task, emotionally draining and, I think, whilst it's great to power on and get things done and make things happen, we've also got to be tender with ourselves during that upheaval and allow ourselves to see the size of it. Not to wallow in it necessarily but just to give ourselves the kind words and the pat on the back that we need, as if to say: 'You're doing a great job, keep going."

Helen Massy has been a military spouse for almost 20 years and, as well as moving around the UK, she's spent time in the Falklands and Canada. She runs a business as a medical health writer. We spoke on the podcast whilst she was living in Canada, which is where she launched *Career Pursuit* – a magazine that informs military partners and veterans about employment and self-employment.

"I was a physiotherapist and a clinical specialist in respiratory disease in the NHS for over ten years and, when we moved around the UK, I found jobs in my specialty and took it for granted that I would be able to work in a different country just as easily. But it's not possible in Canada due to their regulations. That meant that I had to think outside the box and set up a new business.

Launching Career Pursuit came from my own personal experience. When you get posted abroad, especially when you're the only Brits in a particular location, you don't get the same support that you get from the UK bases and it's really hard to find career support. I did reach out to several sources in the UK but there was no one-stop shop to find all of the information. I would get dribs and drabs of knowledge on writing a CV and tips on things to do but it took months to find out anything. I actually ended up reaching out to the US, who had created a similar publication to Career Pursuit, and I ended up writing an article for them. They really have an extensive support network for their military spouses. It was really easy to find the information in the United States but I was living in Canada and wasn't sure where to go. After months and months of research, I found out there are so many great resources in the UK, so many available things for military spouses to access, so I just wanted to put it all in one place. I didn't want other people to go through all of that research to find out where it all was. And that's how Career Pursuit was born.

Something that stuck out to me was that I was told a lot of the time just to 'get any job'. But I didn't want just to go and get a random position somewhere. I have a specialist career; a career that I'd built for over ten years and, as a result, a lot of skills that I wanted to share. That tends to be the first line when trying to get spouses into jobs – just get any job. To steal a line from Jaime Chapman, who supports US military spouses in finding employment: 'It's about careers, not jobs.' They are making sure that those skills are recognised and helping people set up their own businesses or helping people succeed and have something they can take with them wherever they go, rather than just getting a quick job that isn't really going to satisfy you or utilise your skills.

Geographically, it's always been a challenge in the US because they can't translate jobs as easily from state to state so, even working as a clinician or teacher, their qualifications aren't necessarily transferable. I think they've had to deal with this problem from the beginning. In comparison, it's a little bit easier in the UK to often move around with the job, so it's taken for granted that you don't have to re-qualify. They still have the same problems in the US but many more companies have got on board to offer remote work to their serving spouses. I think that many more online remote-working jobs are available in the private sector and that's only really coming to fruition now in the UK. If anything, I know that the pandemic has been a hindrance but, in some ways, it's helped prove that those remote working options are now becoming available.

And what are Helen's best tips for finding clients when posted abroad?

"I would say you don't need to look on your doorstep. Instead, reach out to the UK, Canada and the United States and get support from all three countries with a wealth of information. That's why I think reaching beyond your doorstep is a great thing to do. It's a global world. That sounds like a silly phrase but it's a small world now. You can have clients anywhere, work with clients anywhere and make your business much bigger than the client base you find on your doorstep."

And that's so true for those who might face an international posting or perhaps even for all of us. We live in a truly global world and your business should take advantage of that as much as possible. Because, you never know, there could be a day when you get a posting notice for somewhere much further than the UK.

19

HOW TO KEEP RUNNING A BUSINESS THROUGH A MILITARY DEPLOYMENT

"Distance is not for the fearful, it's for the bold.
It's for those who are willing to spend a lot of time alone
in exchange for a little time with the one they love.
It's for those who know a good thing when they see it,
even if they don't see it nearly enough."

– Meghan Daum. American author

When your partner goes away on deployment, it can be one of the hardest things you can experience in your military life – both emotionally and for your business.

We've had so many deployments throughout our marriage and our relationship – there was, of course, Iraq that rolled into Afghanistan and humanitarian deployments to Nepal and the Caribbean. I think my husband has probably spent four years altogether out of the country. It has been tough!

I spoke before about how I have built my business as a reaction to our transient military life but now I want to go into some detail about how I've done it during a deployment.

There are some really crummy parts of deployments. First up, I want to discuss the most significant issue – isolation.

The big issue I have always had is the isolation of deployments. As someone who's always experienced them alone, quite often at the beginning of a new posting, I am frighteningly aware of how painful that isolation can be and the damage it can cause to one's mental health.

When I interviewed the lovely Georgie for the podcast, we touched on how isolation – in this case, during the pandemic – can really affect how you function and the ways in which you can help ease it.

"I think the biggest thing [about deployments] is this sense of disconnection and loneliness. For the first few weeks, things are suppressed and you can numb it with TV, sugar, alcohol, shopping, endless FaceTime calls to friends or just sort of scrolling through your phone – we can numb it out.

But those systems, sadly, only hold back what we're really feeling for so long and we all know that they are detrimental in the long term – they're not great for us, either physically, emotionally or health-wise.

So firstly, it's just acknowledging if you are feeling lonely or disconnected and that this is really rubbish for you, at the moment. See it because then we can start to support it. And really get clear on what it is that you're missing. This 'what' is going to be so individual.

A lady I was chatting to in my coaching group on Facebook said: 'I just miss you – all I want is a hug.' We all feel that. We just want a hug. That physical touch may be a physical thing but it also creates an emotional response. What I encouraged her to do was to see that it was probably a physical component that she was craving. I also asked her to think about what that physical touch and hug meant to her emotionally and, when we dug into it, it was about reassurance. It was about safety. And it was about feeling supported.

It was then that we thought: 'okay, so the real goal here is not just a hug – the real goal is physical touch, feeling supported, safe and reassured.' From here, we can look at other avenues that might provide similar feedback emotionally and a similar result.

Now, it's not going to be the same for everyone but it might just help us move from nothing to some of it. So, for example, the reassurance. That reassurance was about feeling as if we [as a couple] are still in this together; we might be apart but I love you. That's when you could say: 'I really could do with a hug because I want to know that we're still in this together.' You ask for that reassurance more verbally than you would perhaps ask for it physically if your partner were around.

So you start to look at what is behind what it is you are really missing. What is the feeling? And how can you explore – and 'explore' is the key – lots of different ways that might give you an ounce of what you're craving. It's about knowing how you can do that in your days, little by little, just topping it up bit by bit and welcoming it into your life when you work out what that is. What feels a bit like a warm hug to you? Perhaps your favourite home-cooked meal can feel like a warm hug or your favourite blanket on the sofa can feel safe, protective and comforting.

It's about connecting with all these little things that just pour into those little buckets that are empty because you're missing your partner whilst they're away, which they would typically pour into and what they usually contribute to filling. It's not about becoming self-reliant and so self-resilient that you don't need them anymore. It's about supporting yourself as best you can in the situation you find yourself in, bringing the little joys in new ways and giving to yourself whilst they're away."

Isolation is probably the most painful part of any deployment. You can be in a room full of people but still feel alone and miss your significant other. The pain of missing someone should never be underestimated and, looking back, the pain of attending yet another wedding or party without my husband still hurts my heart a little bit, even now. We've missed countless birthdays, anniversaries and events, and, alongside the longing to see them is the fear that something might happen to them whilst they're away.

But, despite all of this, there are a lot of positives for the entrepreneurial side of me. Don't get me wrong, deployments, detachments, tours... they all SUCK, no matter what you decide to call them. But there are a few positives that you can add to the mix.

THE GOOD BITS OF DEPLOYMENT

Now, aside from sleeping like a starfish and watching whatever you like on the telly, deployments have other benefits that can greatly help your business.

You can ultimately be 100% selfish and focus on your business. Yes, that's right. You no longer need to please anyone else or catch up with box sets in the evenings. Instead, you get to pick when and where you work on your business, whenever you fancy.

Perhaps, if you have the capacity, a deployment is the time to get stuck into a really big project. One that turns your house or life on its head and that you wouldn't usually get away with if your partner was around. Perhaps that might be launching your business (if you haven't already).

I've met many business owners who've picked a deployment as a time to start their businesses, using the time and their partner's return date as a deadline to get it all going. You can suddenly find yourself in complete control of how you spend your time so why not fill that with something you want to do? Doing something like this helps to keep you distracted from constantly counting down the days and it also gives you something to get excited about and share with your partner if and when you get to talk to them during their time away.

Yes, it's always nice to have someone to bounce your new ideas off of but, if you're anything like me, you might find that you speak to your partner even more when they're away. Life seems to get in the way when my husband is here and we often fall into the routine of watching TV and not saying much to each other in the evenings when he is around. But, when he's deployed (and contactable), we have proper focused time when we talk to one another and what better thing to talk about than your shiny new business or project? Not only will it avoid those awkward silences when they can't talk about what they're doing where they are but it also means that you can get excited about your business or project together, so they aren't missing out.

Plus, there are only so many times you can listen to them talking about their job, and now you get to share your career plans, too. My husband loves it when he calls home to hear that I have been busy and am excited about work – I sometimes wonder if he worries that I am too lonely without him but he's soon reassured when he knows that I am busy.

HOW TO RUN A BUSINESS WHEN YOUR PARTNER RETURNS FROM DEPLOYMENT

And then, the big day arrives when they come home! You might have been desperate for them to return but there's a whole load of unexpected challenges that can happen once they are back. Suddenly, you feel the need to make up the time and start to do things together. This probably means that you might want to stop working for a while – brilliant! Self-employment works perfectly in this situation. If you have planned out your workload, you can take that time off.

Most deployments come with a few days or weeks of POT/DL (post operational tour/deployment leave), which can be lovely. You get to spend quality time together and share even more information about what you have been doing whilst they've been away. You can even rope them into testing your new product or service, and there's nothing handier than a fresh pair of eyes to look through your new website or help you with your early ideas.

However, if post-operational leave drags on and you are keen to get back to work, you might suddenly feel like your partner is getting under your feet. This is because your business and work life will probably have changed dramatically since they went away, which can cause a lot of conflicts.

Communication is really key here. If you've experienced any deployment, you'll both know that life doesn't stop when they go away and things at home will change. They even used to get taught that when they used to have their decompression. Yep, they used to have to remind serving personnel that just because they used to do things one way before they left, it doesn't necessarily mean it'll be the same when they get home, so it's important to understand that your new business life might take some getting used to for your newly returned partner. Just keep talking. My ways to avoid conflicts are to have conversations from the start, a dedicated office space and specific working hours. If your partner knows where you'll be and when you'll be there, you can work out the best system for both of you moving forwards.

So, there we have it, my best tips for running your business through military deployments and in those first tricky weeks after they return. I hope they have helped you understand how it's possible and not all bad. Yes, deployments are SO rubbish but they are an inevitable part of this life that we find ourselves partnered with. Facing them with an action plan and a business to focus on can speed up the deployment and make the whole thing a lot less painful.

20

RUNNING A BUSINESS WITH CHILDREN
(YES, EVEN THE FURRY, FOUR-LEGGED KIND)

"In the end, I've realised that legacy is not important
except to your children and family and friends.
When I am on my deathbed, I just want to feel as if I have
loved and been loved, done some good in the world,
and made a difference here and there."

– Sir Richard Branson. English business magnate, investor and author

As I touch on later in this book, it's important to never take business advice from people who haven't got their own business, so it would be foolish of me to now start giving advice on something I have such little experience in! As I write this my baby has just turned one, and I've only just returned from maternity leave. That is why I have asked some of my favourite parents to contribute to this next chapter.

There are lots of families within our military community who have children, so I think it's important for me to add this chapter. If you do have children, it's a good time to consider how they might fit into your self-employment plans.

Also, I must stress that even though the majority of Milspos I meet are mums, there's still a lot of goodness in this chapter for everyone, so do have a read through even if you don't have children. I think you'll be able to gain a lot from it.

First up, we have lovely Nadine from Forces Family Finance. Nadine is one of those amazing women that just gets her head down to create the kind of business that we all dream of! One that can pay a decent salary as well as support the family when it comes to living the post-military life.

As mentioned in the previous section, Nadine started her business when her children were tiny. Despite its challenges, she now runs an exceptional business (Honestly, you really should check it out!). Here's how she did it:

"A lot of the time when you've got young children, you pretty much plan around their routine, such as nap times and the bedtime routine.

My start point was always: okay so these are the needs of my children and the things that I have to do for that, and then I added my work tasks and the things that I needed to do around that, rather than trying to do it the other way around. Because ultimately, you're almost setting yourself up for failure if you don't pick your children's needs first. Things don't always go to plan but you have to be alright with it and not beat yourself up about it too much."

But, as Nadine continues, here's the key to succeeding in business with small children and it's something that, as a child of an entrepreneur, I completely agree with.

"I also think about the example that I'm setting for my children as well. I've asked them so many times 'Would you prefer it if Mummy worked for somebody else but then I wouldn't be there on the school run or to do those things? Or do you want me to do this?' and every time they say, 'No Mum, you do your business.' I see myself inspiring them, which is amazing."

In series three of *The InDependent Spouse* podcast, I spoke to Dr

Gillian Jones about the importance that self-employment gives her role within her family. Gill is a military artist who, after leaving the Navy, became chronically ill. Her business gives her the space to express herself, all whilst being able to provide for her family. We spoke about how vital showing your children the importance of working is and how, for Gill, self-employment was flexible enough to fit around her challenges.

Jess Sands:
"So, my mum is disabled – I've spoken about this before – she has multiple sclerosis but, when we were children, she ran her own business from home, which I think, gosh, it's probably her fault that I'm now doing this! But it was really quite an inspiring thing to see my mum slogging away, working really hard despite her disability, and achieving really big things and being a role model for me – I think that's really important for our children to see."

Gillian Jones:
"I was training to be a teacher a few years ago and that involved dropping the kids off at wraparound care first thing in the morning, before dashing off and not coming back 'til 6 o'clock and then working until midnight. It was during that period that I started to get unwell, really unwell, and I had to give it up, which was awful as I'd always wanted to be a teacher. It was my long-term plan, after I'd done the Navy, to do that. But, once I got over the fact that it was awful (I'm still working on it but getting there), and decided to focus on this, I've seen so much difference in my children – they're so much more open with me. They put up with the fact that I have to go to bed and just come and hug me and have a chat at the end of the day and will cook their own dinner when I can't.

So, although there are massive downsides to it all, there are upsides as well and that sort of learning of empathy and of fitting one's life around what you're capable of doing. I think it's quite a good lesson for the kids and I think it's the same in any military family – you have to learn to fit your life around the circumstance.

My husband doesn't go away that much but we've got a different issue to fit around, a different circumstance to fit around. So it's all sort of a learning and growing opportunity."

ADDING CHILDREN TO YOUR BUSINESS LIFE

Then there are times where you might already be an experienced business owner and have just received the exciting news that you are going to have a baby!

I spoke to my pal, psychologist Dr Rosie Gilderthorp, who specialises in helping parents within the military community. She's a Navy wife who has a wealth of experience in mental health support and I was lucky enough to interview her for the podcast. She understands that, even at the very start, when you become a new parent you might need that extra bit of support to help keep your head above water.

"Military families need that extra help because of the lack of connection with the rest of your life. So, when we're looking at mental health, it's really important that we don't think that it's just about what goes on in our head. Because it's not. It's about a whole range of things, a whole package and a big part of that package is connection with other people and meaningful activity in your life.

And a lot of the important things that we lose – every time we move or when we face a big life change (like a partner going on deployment where our childcare and support network changes) – are these connections. It's when, seemingly overnight, everything has changed and suddenly life looks entirely different – they almost can't find themselves within that.

It's a story I've heard so many times and that is the reason that we struggle more with our mental health."

I've been in postings before where I've had some lovely friends, who have just had babies, come knocking at my door in floods of tears because they just can't work it out. My first thought is always that they're coming to someone who has no experience with children. If you've ever found yourself in a similar situation and you're not sure who to turn to, Dr Rosie has some really great advice to get you through those struggles.

"The first thing is to make some genuine connections. There's a lot that you can do to enhance your mental health at that time but, actually, the most powerful thing you can do is have a genuine talk with another human being who cares about you.

The way that our minds work is actually very basic. Your brain is constantly asking 'Am I safe or am I not safe?' If you don't feel safe, your fight or flight system is activated and, when that's activated, everything feels very difficult when you're dealing with a baby. We get overwhelmed really easily because this is a part of our brain that is only actually designed for fighting off tigers or running away. You can't run away from your baby (and you probably shouldn't fight with it either) so that part of your brain doesn't know what to do and just finds the whole world incredibly overwhelming.

On top of that, it gives you symptoms such as being unable to sleep, being agitated or being on edge all the time. It might even send you into depression because it wants you to stay safe and not run the risk of a predator seeing you as weak. So it tries to keep you really safe and small in your house, making it really hard for you to even imagine going outside. These are all things the brain does because it thinks that you're not safe. That's why we need to show it that you are safe and to do that we have to activate a different part of the brain, which (in compassion focus therapy) we call the soothing system – it's *the part that does all of the resting and digesting and connecting with other people.*

What you really need is just somebody to listen to you, be kind towards you, smile at you and provide you with some basics like food, and all of that stuff communicates safety to the brain. Then you'll get a bit of head space and you can work on the rest of the stuff that's going to help you but if you don't have that feeling of being supported, none of the other stuff's going to make much difference.

It's genuinely no more complicated than that but it's very rare to find. One of the reasons people really struggle in pregnancy and the postnatal period is that the whole world has an opinion. Everybody wants to tell you what their pregnancy was like, everyone wants to do a one-upmanship. It's just the way our brains are programmed to survive in the pack – blame that survival system, again.

If you are reading this and don't have children but you feel a bit scared about how to support somebody who tells you that they're struggling with their newborn or during pregnancy, remember the stuff above. It's the genuine listening, giving them space – no one wants advice anyway – letting them be who they are and how giving them a biscuit (if you're face-to-face) is really helpful."

The lovely Chris Keen is a freelance radio presenter who I first spoke to when I interviewed him for the podcast back in 2020. Married to Army officer Kelly, Chris was a stay-at-home parent to baby Holly at the time. In the episode, he talked about how he juggles life as a full-time parent caring for Holly at home combined with his self-employed career.

"I'm actually really unorganised but my wife, Kelly, is really organised. So, she's got me a diary and I put everything in it because I'm literally doing six days a week now of radio stuff – whether that's podcasts

or interviews or actual shows – and, on top of that, Holly is in the equation. She gets up at like 5:30–6:30am every day, so I can gauge when her naps are going to be. I know between 9 and 10am and midday, I can whack in an interview or record the radio show.

I'm doing four radio shows a week – all pre-recorded – but I know that I can record two in one day and then the other two on the next. So, they're all out the way at the start of the week and then I can concentrate on other interviews or looking after Holly, going into soft play areas and such.

But there's so much going on and there's things being added to it constantly. I love being busy, I hate being bored so I wouldn't have it any other way at the moment – I really have got the best of both worlds. I loved being in radio full-time but I also love being at home with my family – being able to do radio at home with my family is amazing."

And that's the whole point to it really, isn't it? Family and the flexibility to fit around them so that you can create something they can be proud of, too. For me, as the daughter of someone who ran their own business whilst my dad went out to work, it's given me a greater understanding of the importance of money and hard work. A gift that has helped me more than my mum could ever have known.

So, if you are a parent considering entrepreneurship, I hope you are inspired by these inspirational Milspos and the work that they are doing. They are all creating amazing businesses that are financially viable, inspiring their children and helping others to do the same.

There are so many incredible parents out there running their own businesses… and quite successfully, too. Lots of them have taken part in *The InDependent Spouse* podcast.

So, there's absolutely no reason why you can't start your own business and live that flexible and joyful lifestyle you've always dreamed of. After all, you've got this wonderful book to help you and there are also plenty of incredible networks out there that will support you along your journey.

21

MY POWER YEAR

"Keep good company, read good books, love good things
and cultivate soul and body as faithfully as you can."
– Louisa May Alcott. American novelist, short story writer and poet,
best known as the author of the novel Little Women

I wrote this down the other day whilst I was on hold…

Military life is meant to be tough and military wives are
meant to be resilient. That's just how it is meant to be – but is
that REALLY true? There's surely got to be another way.

You see, the thing is that when I moved to my last posting (just before I lived where I am now), I HATED it! As in, I truly hated it. Now, I always do my best to find the positives in life but I really, really hated it. I hated the noise of the traffic, the fact that everyone had been there longer and was settled, I hated that the house was so dark, I hated that I was so far away from 'home' and I hated that the garden was tiny and dead… and I mean yellow-grass, drier-than-dry-soil dead. We moved to Central London at the start of August into what can only be described as a teeny tiny dust-bowl dark house – think Miss Havisham's house but without the character and a lot of MAGNOLIA.

It was over 35 degrees on the day we moved and it stayed that hot for two whole weeks! I had moved from a leafy-green country posting with beautiful summers to sweaty, grotty Central London, smack bang in the middle of a heatwave and I hated every moment of it.

For the first two weeks, every morning after my husband left for work, I would look at the dog – who would often look back at me with the same expression – and we would wonder how the hell we'd gotten ourselves into this mess. Then, we'd open the back door and the poor dog would just look out, wondering who stole the grass and what that awful racket was. I'd head out into the boiling hot garden with this sad-looking dog and be unable to hear myself think over all the traffic. What was I doing here? I don't like this at all! I like greenery, the countryside, space, fresh air and, well... grass, apparently!

'I'm going to give it six months,' I thought. Six months and then I can leave because I would have given it a go for six whole months and I will have 'tried really hard'. Except, the reality was, that deep inside, I wasn't giving anything a go. I wasn't even trying in the slightest. So, as September arrived and people asked me how we were getting along, my reply was always: "Well, at least I am one month down, only five more to go," as if it were a deployment! I was quite literally wishing my life away.

Don't get me wrong, there have been postings in the past that I have not been so keen on, plus the first few months anywhere new is always a bit difficult. But I have never hated anywhere that much. This was a very new feeling for me and I didn't like it.

I like to subscribe to the fact that we are one of a kind and are so lucky to have even made it to this point in our lives, so we owe the world our very best. To fulfil our greatest potential or, at the very least, be as happy as we can be. Hating something that I hadn't even tried to enjoy was against my every belief of what I wanted. So, it was time to shake it up! It was time to look at things differently, drag myself out of this doom and stop wishing the days away.

But first, I had to own it. I had to acknowledge that this was my choice and that I was not here because I was dragged, bound and gagged by a posting order but because I had come to this decision on my own. Now, my decision had to be accepted and changed, not to compromise or blame anyone, but to own it truly. This is my life and these are my life choices.

> *"The last of one's freedoms is to choose*
> *one's attitude in any given circumstance."*
>
> *– Viktor E. Frankl. Jewish-Austrian psychiatrist who founded logotherapy*

Let me tell you about Fiona Stanford.

When I interviewed author Fiona Stanford for the podcast series, it had a lasting effect on me. Fiona and her husband have had 17 quarters in 25 years of military service. Can you believe that... 17 houses!? Fiona has given up jobs, left friends behind, moved countries and sacrificed more than we could ever know for this Armed Forces life. But, the one thing I will never forget, is when we talked 'off-air' after the recording.

Fiona realised early on that she could no longer blame her husband for his career and the many moves they had encountered because of it. Her opinion and the resentment around all those goodbyes were no longer serving her. Fiona realised that the only constant through all of the postings was her and her husband, and they were a team. And, the only way to get through it and be happy doing it, was to act as a team. She had to own the fact that she had chosen this life – it wasn't thrust upon her by force, so blaming her husband would just make it all much more painful and not even slightly change the circumstances.

Polly Charnley, from The Be Glad Movement, does something similar:

"The Be Glad Movement is a collection of stories that are based on good things coming out of bad situations and reasons to be glad. The reason I started this project revolves around my name. Basically, my mum named me Pollyanna after the book and film Pollyanna.

For those of you who aren't familiar with this story, Pollyanna is a little orphan who gets sent off to live with her slightly mean auntie. Her dad taught her to play 'the glad game' – looking for positives in every negative situation. My mum really loved this film, which is why she named me Pollyanna.

When I was growing up, if ever anything went wrong in my life or I had a setback, my mum would say to me, 'Now come on, Polly, play the glad game,' and I would have to list off everything that I was grateful for or lucky to have in my life. It's a strategy that has served me well over the years. She didn't do this to belittle whatever I was going through but to help me refocus and see the good instead."

I knew at that moment exactly what had to be done. I had to own my decisions, I had to own my choices and I had to own my response to this new posting.

But I had to make sure that I gave myself the best stab at it. The reality was that I was still living in London, in a very dark house, with a very dead and noisy garden – a bit of a challenge for someone who loves space and nature – so that had its challenges. But, to give myself the best possible chance of changing my view to one of positivity, I had to look after myself inside and out, and jump into this new posting with both feet! So, I embarked on a power year!

My power year would be a year of soaking up things that inspired me, reframing my outlook, taking care of myself and becoming my most successful self. It was also about investing time in the tools that would help me. And, finally, to give me the best chance of making the most of this new, yet awkward, posting.

As the children returned to school in the first week of September, I embarked on my attempt at my power year. I told myself that, from now on, I wasn't going to allow myself to hate this posting. Instead, I would seek out and capture every opportunity that this two-and-a-half-year posting could give me. Here's what I learnt...

FIRST UP, THE BASICS –
SLEEP, FOOD, WATER AND EXERCISE

I cannot stress the importance of looking after yourself when you run your own business. Unlike a traditional company with a team that has your back, when starting, you will tend to be going solo. That means that if you can't work in your business due to ill health, regardless of whether it is physical or mental, your business will grind to a halt.

That's why decent amounts of sleep, nutritious food, water and exercise are the basics here and, I know we've heard it a thousand times but, you really shouldn't underestimate how valuable these basics are. Not just because it makes good health sense but because it makes good business sense, too.

And that was what I focused on. I bought myself one of those mega two-litre water bottles and drank from that daily. I signed up for a fitness app and sweated around my (still dark but more positive-feeling) front room every few days. I bought new pillows, comfy PJs, lavender sleep spray and new bedsheets. I was determined to give myself the best fighting chance to feel as good as possible; to provide myself with the best foundations to build my power year.

Now that I had my personal foundations laid down, it was time to build my business foundations and my mindset.

MY POWER YEAR TOOLS

BUSINESS MEDITATION

I am sure you've heard of meditation and probably had a go at it, too, or perhaps it's already built in place and you're a daily meditator. Fab, isn't it? Meditation can help reduce stress, bring mindfulness or work to calm you before a big event. But did you know there are guided meditations specifically for business?

In guided meditations, the meditation itself is shaped by another person's voice. Our minds tend to wander, which is why there is guidance, so that it has something to focus on in our bid to help change inner thoughts or expectations. This can sometimes take the form of live guidance in a group setting or through the use of pre-recorded meditations shared via apps, podcasts and videos.

For businesses, guided meditations usually focus on confidence, manifestation and visualisations, like we covered before, or letting go of previous issues that may be affecting your success in moving forwards.

There are hundreds, if not thousands, of business coaches offering guided mediation for business but don't let that put you off. I would personally recommend the app Calm and start using its daily meditations. They are loosely guided and a great starting point to get you into regular meditation. Once you become used to the practice, perhaps head over to someone like Tony Robbins or Abigail Rogers to see what they are offering or, better still, why not record your own?

I strive to meditate every day for at least 15 minutes. At first, it felt strangely uncomfortable, distracting and frustrating. But slowly, as time progressed, it became part of my routine and something I now look forward to.

BUSINESS JOURNALING
(OR KEEPING A BUSINESS DIARY)

I guess this one is sort of self-explanatory. It's pretty much a diary but, rather than writing about your personal day, you write about your business day – what you achieved, what went wrong and any plans you might have for the future.

When I started mine on the advice of a friend, it sounded like a complete waste of time. I thought, *'What is the point of writing about something that's already happened? Can I really learn anything from this?'*

But the reality is that when you take a step back from your business and reassess what's gone well and what hasn't, it can provide you with a clear overview of it all. It's also brilliant to look back on and appreciate how much you have achieved as well as serving as an even better place to write your big goals for the future of your business.

So, what's the harm in giving it a go for yourself? Grab a notebook or treat yourself to a shiny new one* and write about how today has been when it comes to your business. You might not like it at first and it might not last all that long, but please, give it a go. You never know, you might be pleasantly surprised by how much you enjoy and benefit from it!

I now journal most working days – I use it as a way to look back on all I have achieved but it mostly helps me to work out how I could solve any problems that unexpectedly pop up. I especially enjoy looking back over everything at the end of the year or at points when running a business feels tough, as a way to remind myself just how much I've achieved... even if it doesn't feel like it.

SURROUNDING YOURSELF WITH INSPIRATION

That married quarter "home" I mentioned earlier on in this chapter was truly depressing. It was soulless! There was too much magnolia – if that's even possible – and, as a result, I was feeling drab and uninspired, which is where a little bit of inspiration was needed.

This one is simple. What you put in, you tend to get out. You can apply it to most things but this example is about mindset and both being and staying inspired. For my power year, I was going to make an active decision to engage in inspirational content. This meant books, podcasts, social media and television; not just adding to my intake but also removing negativity from the content I was experiencing on a daily basis.

The basic principle was that if it didn't inspire me or it made me feel bad, then I no longer watched, read or engaged with it. So, *Real Housewives of Somewhere or Other* was replaced with TED talks on YouTube, inspirational business owners replaced fake celebs and influencers on Instagram, and trashy magazines were swapped for inspirational books – but, it wasn't all restrictive, there was still a place for some easy TV, too (I can't miss *Strictly!*). Still, the things that made me feel bad, not good enough or were just not that inspirational were removed.

It changed my whole outlook. I no longer felt like I was behind everyone else or not as valuable as others, and I quickly realised that I was achieving the goals I had set out for my business. It helped with my procrastination and just gave me a more positive outlook overall.

CREATING A DREAM BOARD OR GOAL BOARD

A dream board is a visual representation of all your dreams and desires. These could be business dreams or personal ones – it's completely up to you. It's something that you look at every day that will inspire you to achieve your dreams and goals. It might sound like a strange thing to do but, believe me, it works!

My dream board Is quite simply a pinboard. Each 'Twixmas' (those days between Christmas and New Year when you aron't 100% sure what day it is!) or at the start of January, I take myself off to a cosy corner of the house with a cuppa. I light a candle and start dreaming about what I really want to achieve in the coming year and beyond. It ranges from having more members in the Milspo community to writing this book and going on that holiday of a lifetime. After that, I sit down with my computer and find visual representations of those goals. I edit screenshots of the members' community to show the numbers I am aiming for; I create a mock-up of my book cover and an invite to my book launch and find a beautiful image of my dream holiday destination. Then I print them off, add them to my pinboard and mount it proudly next to my desk so that I see it all every day... somewhere I know I won't be able to miss it!

My board really comes into its own about mid-February when it is still grotty outside and things are starting to feel sluggish. It helps to keep me on track and stay focused whilst allowing me to dream about all of those wonderful things that will happen over the year and why I am doing what I'm doing when it comes to my business.

Most years, I achieve my dreams, stick the images of what I have achieved in my journal and others fall into the following year. Of course, some of my massive dreams have been on my board for longer (like this book), but they are too exciting to give up.

You could start your vision board on Pinterest or as a folder saved on your desktop but there's something about printing them out and looking at them in the physical sense that keeps me going on those gloomy days.

PRIORITISING WHEN YOU'RE OVERWHELMED
(OR, EATING THE FROG AND HIS FRIENDS)

"If the first thing you do in the morning is to eat the frog, then you can continue your day with the satisfaction of knowing that this is probably the worst thing that will happen to you all day."

– *Mark Twain. Late American writer,*
humorist, entrepreneur, publisher and lecturer

Have you ever noticed that you generally have two types of reactions when you're overwhelmed by work and your list of tasks is never-ending? You either tackle the smaller jobs to feel like you're achieving a lot or you procrastinate, binge-watch Netflix, get sucked into Facebook and leave the important tasks to the last minute.

As you've probably experienced, none of this helps you achieve your big goals but there is a way you can avoid this altogether. How? I hear you say? By eating that frog... and some of his friends!

The origin of this saying

Don't panic... I'm not asking you to eat an actual frog! The 'frog' symbolises the task that you least want to do. That's why it's advised to start your day with the most important task that you are also dreading. By doing this, you will feel relieved, and the other tasks will seem more straightforward. I take this one step further by 'eating' his friends, too.

Each day I pick three (or sometimes five) of the most critical tasks and make sure they are my priority. Nothing else on my to-do list can come before them – no getting lost in the social media scroll or the distractions of that next Netflix binge until those tasks are completed. These three tasks are sometimes client work but, usually, they relate to my 'bigger picture' goals and are always a step towards achieving them.

But how can you work out, from your long to-do list, what 'the frog' is? Here's where the Eisenhower Matrix comes in.

THE EISENHOWER MATRIX

	URGENT	NOT URGENT
IMPORTANT	**DO** Do it now	**DECIDE** Schedule a time
NOT IMPORTANT	**DELEGATE** Who can help?	**DELETE** Remove

The Eisenhower Matrix, also called the Urgent-Important Matrix, helps you to decide on and prioritise tasks by urgency and importance, allowing you to identify the less urgent and essential tasks that you should either delegate or just simply not do.

Split your to-do list into the boxes above to help you decide which tasks might be your 'frogs' and which tasks you can leave that little bit longer. This is a working document that will change as new tasks come in.

Once you've worked out a priority, the next step is to schedule it into your day. Of course, you should also be scheduling your lunch break (yes, you do need one), any exercise you would like to complete and any appointments you also need to attend that day.

You can use this process to plan your year, quarter, month or day, and I promise you it will help you be much more productive. For example, having my three or five frogs each day means I stay on track, focus on my goals and achieve something towards them each day.

CELEBRATING THE GOOD STUFF

There's something about running a business that takes over everything, to the point where you are so engrossed that sometimes the good things pass you by in all the chaos. My best pal calls it *'head down, bum up working'*. You work so hard that you don't have a chance to celebrate.

Celebrating my wins is one of the things that I miss from working in a team and one of the reasons we have a weekly celebratory post in the Milspo Network each Friday.

When you work in traditional employment, you usually have a boss checking in on your projects and complimenting you when you've done a good job – at least, that's what we all hope for, right? But, when you're working alone, these moments can be easily missed.

The key is to recognise when you've done a good job and celebrate it. For some, that could be buying yourself something lovely (I have a posh candle obsession), or it could be as simple as taking Friday afternoons off to treat yourself to a coffee. Many business owners I know have a jar on their desk where they add marbles every time they get a new client, or they have an online planner that plays a happy song when they have completed a task. Whatever it is, no matter how small, make sure you recognise and celebrate your achievements. Otherwise, it can be easy to fall into the trap of working away and never feeling like you've got anywhere. It's your business and you are achieving extraordinary things. Make sure you give yourself a well-earned pat on the back!

MAKING THE MOST OF THE COMMUNITY

We covered the power of networking in chapter 8. I realised pretty early on that I had moved and not started networking again. So that's what I added to my power year. I networked in real life and online, and rebuilt my business the way I wanted it to be. It took a little while but, before long, I had re-established my network and had a collection of people, both within and outside the military community, with whom I could connect and share business knowledge with. I especially paid attention to my online connections, those posted worldwide, because I knew that my life would involve more postings in the future.

———

The truth is that for your business, and maybe even for yourself, the location of your posting doesn't actually matter. What matters is your response to it. I knew if I could combine a different outlook with the tools I knew had already achieved good results, I could change my mentality and thrive in this posting that I hated so much. I am the driving force behind my business and, because I was now filling my cup, my business was no longer suffering. I found that I had new clients and better work. I was more inspired to grow Milspo and I was much happier.

But life is not perfect. You will fall off the wagon – I have done this a few times and I often find myself reassessing and realigning in January after the chaos of Christmas. But that's okay. Like everything, just because you didn't stick to something for one moment, day, week or even year, doesn't mean you have to just give up. You can just start again. YOU get to decide how you respond to any situation, and hopefully, from now on, it will be with passion and the tools in your pocket to create your own power year.

**REMEMBER – YOU HAVE THE FREEDOM TO CHOOSE
YOUR ATTITUDE TO ANY CIRCUMSTANCE.**

So, to sum up this chapter, my power year consisted of:

Sorting out the basics, drinking enough water, prioritising good food and scheduling exercise. I added daily meditations and time for journaling to my day. I surrounded myself with inspiration and created my own goal board as a visual reminder of everything I wanted to achieve. I connected with a community of fantastic business owners and I remembered to celebrate with them when things went well. And then, most importantly, I was gentle with myself when things didn't go exactly to plan. I remembered that I have complete control over how I chose to react to each circumstance, which made a massive difference to me and my business.

* If you're anything like me, you'll know there's nothing better than a new notepad. That little warm, fuzzy feeling you get from writing on the first page of a clean, untouched book, one that's ready to be filled with amazingness! Pure joy!

22

COLLABORATION OVER COMPETITION

"Always be a first-rate version of yourself
instead of a second-rate version of somebody else."
– *Judy Garland. American actor, singer, vaudevillian and dancer*

There's something very important in business that I believe is the quickest way to grow a successful company. Yet it seems to be something that is rather difficult for so many business owners to get their heads around – collaborating with others, especially if they are in the same industry as you.

WHAT DO I MEAN BY COLLABORATION?

Collaboration is when you partner up with another small business owner so that you both reach the same end goal. That might be a joint event, running a shared community or simply making an arrangement that you'll pass on overspill clients to them.

Usually, these people will work in the same industry as you, doing something that complements your work or, ideally, someone who does exactly the same line of work.

But I see these people as my competition! Surely, I can't work
WITH them?! They'll steal all of my ideas and customers.

There's always a hesitance to engage with your competition when thinking about your business, especially if you've previously had to deal with mean girls or copycats who have pissed you off (for lack of a better phrase!).

I have had loads of people copy me since I started my business and the Milspo Network – and, even now, it surprises me every time!

I used to spend hours getting angry and so annoyed at them. How dare they do this to me? Why couldn't they think of their own ideas? Why were they doing exactly what I was doing?!

I spent so much time stressing and worrying and, do you know what? It distracted me from what really mattered – my own business.

You see, business is like a swimming race. The most successful people swim their little hearts out in their own lane. They're using their best swim stroke. They've trained for it, focused on their timing and rhythm, and they are successful. But it's that moment when they get distracted and turn to look at what others are doing, that they lose their concentration, go off balance and start to flounder. The secret to swimming your best race in business is to just stay focused on your own lane.

When I get copied now, I mostly get confused by these people. I can never understand why you would want to be a copycat. The real joy when you run your own business is the success that comes from your own ideas and achievements. Surely if that's someone else's ideas, you haven't achieved anything – you are quite literally a cheap copy of the person you've, well, copied. What a waste of potential!

I can promise you now that those copycats will NEVER succeed in business. They are followers who are at least two or three weeks behind everyone else. You, dear reader, are better than that. You don't want to be a follower. You want to be a leader! And by genuinely embracing the idea of collaboration rather than competition, you will find that success flowing to you.

I know it can be hard to trust people and I understand that you still might not be convinced, but here's the thing...

When you open yourself up to the idea that those who work in the same field as you are not your competitors and see them as colleagues instead, it means that not only do you remove that feeling of anger but you also open yourself up to collaboration and, in turn, greater success.

You will succeed in business because you chose to do it in the best possible way. Not by being a cheap, angry copycat focusing on someone else. You will be your unique and sparkling self, building your amazing business!

OKAY, LET'S TALK ABOUT COLLABORATION AND HOW IT CAN BENEFIT YOUR BUSINESS

Now that we know the kind of business owner we will be (leader, not a copycat follower, of course), we need to open ourselves up to collaborating.

You probably now have an existing network that you've grown from communities or at networking events, so you'll probably have experienced examples of people collaborating in business. But, before we brainstorm some ideas, let's discuss the reasons why they can help your business.

Collaboration helps your business in a few ways:
- It helps with brand alignment. Collaboration allows your business

to take on the themes of another similar brand, adding the qualities of your collaborator's brand to yours and vise versa.

- You'll gain a bigger audience and access to that company's customers to help sell your own products or services.
- You'll be able to leverage the network of that other company.
- It's half the work and less lonely – there's nothing like running your own business to make you feel lonely and worn out. Collaborate and, in theory, you'll be getting someone else to enjoy the ride with you and gain twice the results.
- Promote their businesses and they'll promote yours – I have found that the more support I give to other people's businesses, the more I get back in return. I don't do it for this reason though; that's just a happy bonus. Any recommendation or referral should always be a two-way street.* Be clear about which businesses you would like to support and promote them accordingly. Doing this often takes a conscious effort but, after a while, it becomes second nature.

HERE ARE SOME OF MY BEST COLLABORATION IDEAS:**

1. **Be an accountability buddy.** Help other business owners achieve their goals by holding them accountable. Partner up and help them work towards achieving their objectives – you'll often find that they'll want to do the same for you, too. Meet up in real life or online at a scheduled time and give each other half the meeting time to review and set new goals. Then, at the next meeting, check how each of you has progressed and decide on the new aims between now and your next meeting.

2. **Become a Business BFF.** It's a lonely life as a solopreneur and military partner. So why not get yourself a Business Best Friend Forever (BFF)? More than an accountability partner, a Business BFF will help you with business, support you when you want to give it all up and celebrate your wins when you succeed! Perfect for when you work alone and miss the company of an office.

3. **Styled shoots.** Whatever this looks like for your industry, getting creative together can make magic happen and it'll also help with

lowering the costs, too. For example, this idea is perfect if you're in the wedding industry and want to showcase your products alongside someone else's.

4. **Co-hosting events.** Maybe you've got the venue and the catering sorted but someone else has the speakers and the products for goodie bags. So, why not join forces to create an amazing event?

5. **Co-founding a business.** This will ultimately bring together your skills, knowledge, contacts, finances, clients and more with another's. But it's crucial that you choose your business partner carefully!

6. **Building a referral network.** Most of my design work comes from referrals or overflow from another designer. If you can find people you trust and direct clients their way, they'll tend to repay the favour.

7. **Video/audio interviews.** Whether featuring on each other's YouTube channels or appearing as guests on each other's podcasts, you're creating new content and giving another perspective and brand input, which will be shared across multiple platforms. Also, similar to the costs, it splits the amount of time you have to spend on creating content.

8. **Guest posting.** Like the interviews above, guest posting is a great way to tap into someone else's audience. This isn't just great for SEO purposes but it does demonstrate a real understanding of a topic and can introduce you to a whole new set of potential clients and customers.

9. **Split support.** This is where the work is shared to achieve the client's goal. If your schedule is too busy or you can't completely fulfil the specification because it's not your area, sometimes it's better to work with someone you trust. For me, that means joining forces with a web designer. I create the designs and they do the technical parts. It means that our client gets an amazing site by using the best skills from the both of us.

10. **Service swapping.** When you're starting out, funds may be limited. A great way to fund your business is through skill swapping.

Perhaps someone out there wants what you do but has the same problem.

COLLABORATION OVER COMPETITION.

Hopefully, now that you're at the end of this chapter, you can see that others you might have previously thought of as competitors could, in fact, be your biggest allies. So take some time now to write down your new potential collaborators in the space below. Add details on how you can get in touch with them and invite them to a one-on-one with you. This could be over coffee, either online or offline. Get to know them. You never know, they could become a big asset to your business.

*Unless it's something you honestly don't like, believe in or wouldn't recommend yourself. In which case, the courteous thing to do is to not accept the positive recommendation or referral. That would just be bad business practice. And, quite frankly, just not a very nice thing to do.

** You can thank me later. Treats are always welcome but a lovely email will make me just as happy!

23

WHAT I LEARNT DURING THE PANDEMIC

"The fastest way to change yourself is to hang out with people who are already the way you want to be."

– Reid Hoffman. LinkedIn co-founder

2020 and 2021 were crazy years! Like me, I think you are probably comfortable with waving 'goodbye' to those long pandemic days and are hopeful for the many possibilities ahead. But, like all things in business, it's important to stop, take a breath and learn from what's happened previously. We have to take away the best experiences but also learn from the least favourable events so that we don't make the same mistakes again.

It's crazy to think, looking back to the start of 2020, that we hadn't even had a chance to get started before it all went that little bit bonkers!

By the start of March, restrictions were imposed; by mid-March, half of Europe had already locked down. On the 23 March, the UK was in total lockdown. We were allowed to go outside for one-hour's exercise each day and could not socialise with other households. For my family, that meant locking down just me, my husband and the dog in our married quarter in Shrivenham.

I wrote the following in my journal…

"It's been one of the weirdest springs in living memory. Terrifying but completely beautiful.

By the end of March, as the weather warmed up, a miracle happened. Colour arrived! In our little corner of Oxfordshire, spring bulbs sprung up in our (quite frankly) boring married quarter garden. Somehow, some years ago, someone had taken the time to plant daffodils, tulips and hyacinths in the drab little bit of green at the front of our house. They literally arrived the same day that we locked down."

And it woke up something within me. Someone had invested in this little corner of the patch with something that would bring joy well after they had left. This person had chosen not to be selfish and plant their bulbs in a pot to take with them when they next had to move but to plant them in the grass at the front of the quarter for everyone to see and enjoy for years to come. They had literally invested in this military community.

The following months saw more miracles like this. Captain Tom walking his 100 laps, UK-wide Thursday-night clapping in the street for our NHS workers and community champions caring for the elderly and those who were struggling financially. Within our military community, things happened, too, as people rose to the challenge that faced the entire world. Members of the Royal British Legion, saddened by the change to the VE Day celebrations that were planned for 8 May 2020, created socially distanced parades throughout the country; hundreds of military spouses volunteered to be NHS first responders so that they could 'serve' alongside their partners, many of whom had been drafted in to support the mass vaccination programme; and wonderful neighbours 'bubbled' together with isolated spouses who were going through deployments alone.

For me, the lockdown was marked by some very special weekly online events – the Milspo Meet-Ups.

One day, just before the UK officially went into lockdown, when things were looking particularly frightening, I popped a random post on the Facebook group asking how everyone was and wondering if they fancied a chat online one day to make sure everyone was coping okay. The replies were vast, with spouses all over the UK and further afield – in countries that were already in lockdown – keen to hear from home.

That very first Milspo Meet-Up, on 18 March 2020, was a very sobering affair. Joined by wives living in Spain and Italy, we had a little glimpse of what was to come in lockdown, which really was frightening to say the least. Many were concerned about the levels that this illness (because it wasn't being called a pandemic at that point) would do to their business and then, more personal things, such as how the military would be involved and how safe they would be during their participation. Would there be civil unrest? Would the military be involved with that? And how on earth would those with partners going through a deployment cope?

What many of us didn't even contemplate at that time would be the damage the pandemic might do to our businesses or the kinds of support there would be, if any, from the MOD or the UK government. Everything was unknown and so worrying.

But, like before, the military community came together and did what it does best: acting like the supportive community it is so good at being. Blitz spirit was back!

In real life, whilst we were sharing flour, pasta and toilet roll online, the Milspo Network met every Wednesday to support, guide and, eventually, once we'd all felt more comfortable about the unbelievable situation that surrounded us, have a really good giggle. Over many weeks, we discussed business, military life, covid restrictions and holiday plans (mostly cancelled ones). But, more importantly, we got isolated spouses through the week, gave overwhelmed mothers a safe space to moan and, for our international friends, somewhere to feel a little bit closer to home.

Two of those who turned up weekly immediately spring to mind when I think back to that time.

Caroline Hocking

Caroline is an accredited accountant who started her business to fit around military life. At the start of lockdown, her husband had just left for a four-month tour in the Falkland Islands. She found herself hundreds of miles away from her family, completely alone, without a partner.

"I found Milspo in early 2020 after leaving my life and career behind to follow my husband. I don't know how I came across Milspo but I am so thankful that I did. I joined the group and decided to log into the virtual networking, even though I was literally shaking with nerves. I have been to many professional networking events where, if you are not part of a group, you are ignored, so I was full of apprehension. I couldn't have been more wrong in my expectations. I came away from the first session delighted with the connections I had made and overjoyed by how friendly and inclusive it was. This spurred me on to join in more and I also started attending the weekly meet-ups, which were so valuable to me.

As I had moved in January 2020, I didn't have any time to really get to know the local area or anyone in it before the pandemic hit. The weekly meet-ups meant that I was not on my own, which was even more important when my husband got deployed. They gave me something social to look forward to and I didn't feel like I ever had to explain myself or my circumstances as everyone already 'got it'. It was also so reassuring talking to everyone else in similar positions who were also trying to navigate business while the world was in a crazy state. I really don't know if I would have handled it all the same if it wasn't for the Milspo Meet-Ups.

I am beyond grateful for all the support and guidance that Jess, Milspo and the wider community has given me, and I can honestly say, hand on heart, that without Milspo I don't think my business would be where it is today!"

It was so lovely to see Caroline each week. Despite being so incredibly lonely and probably quite frightened, we were able to make sure that for those few hours each week, she had company and a safe group of people to talk to.

Dr Gillian Jones

Gillian is a military artist who runs a wonderful company from her studio in Plymouth. Unfortunately, Gill has a lot of health problems, which meant that she went into self-isolation much earlier than we went into lockdown as a whole. I can't even begin to imagine how worried she must have been during that time and yet, there she was each week, embracing what it meant to be a part of the community; if anything, she just loved joining in without having to leave the house.

"Milspo Meet-Ups became the anchor in my week during lockdown. I was shielding, thanks to my dodgy health, and was more than a little worried about getting Covid. All the messaging at that stage was that people with lung conditions were going to have a pretty awful time, so I took shielding very seriously. Milspo Meet-Ups became a place for me to meet a group of people who became colleagues and then friends, and to talk about something other than Covid! We were all trying to work out how to keep our businesses going through the pandemic and the meet-ups were instrumental in keeping us going

on both a practical and emotional level. They really were invaluable during that time and the connections that we all made are still very important. Self-employment can be quite isolating anyway, so having a group of people with whom to share the ups and downs is so important – Covid or no Covid!"

That time was frightening enough without the addition of a health condition. And I can't really imagine how frightening that must have been for Gill. I've never told her this, and no doubt she'll tell me off when she reads this, but I was relieved every time she logged in to our sessions; she is so important to Milspo, and to me personally. Knowing that she was okay for another week somehow made it all feel better. It was so much more than an online business meet-up.

I loved those meet-ups. Finally, there was time for me to talk to other humans who got just how bloody hard life was then, without judgement or jealousy. For someone who suddenly found themselves isolated in a completely different way to what I had experienced before, those meetings were my safe space. Somewhere I could go just to be me. To giggle and talk and feel the support of our community, no matter where they were in the world. Through those six months, we all genuinely made friends for life and I am so proud of what we, as a network, were able to achieve together.

From the initial panic of Covid-19 to the enduring days of furlough and working from home, the military spouse, partner and other-half business community really dug deep during this time and it's made such a lasting difference.

As we leave those pandemic days behind, I can't help but look back because, you know what? It wasn't all that bad.

The whole business community learnt the importance of being able to 'pivot!'. Together, we all found the joy of connecting online with other people from around the world, who we wouldn't necessarily have gotten the chance to meet in the "normal", non-pandemic world. For those in the military community, taking businesses online not only helped them to survive a pandemic but also enabled them to fit it in more flexibly with the military way of life. And, for me, I learnt the fundamental importance of community and how it was able to help me during those tough times. I hope the Milspo Meet-Ups also helped others, especially those who found themselves more isolated than ever before.

The biggest take away from that time was the strength of community and how important it is for military partners in business. And, even now, I think communities are a huge part of helping my own business as well as my personal life.

COMMUNITIES AND HOW THEY ARE ESSENTIAL FOR PERSONAL AND BUSINESS LIFE

Those lockdown meet-ups became greater than traditional networking; it was supporting people who, despite all living through a terrifying time, would become friends.

Those friends are now a whole network of supporters that I can tap into for years to come – be they people I can directly work with or cheerleaders telling the world about what I do (and, as previously discussed, vice versa). This is what you get from investing in a community. We may no longer be in a lockdown but you can leverage this type of support from a community.

The communities you join might not necessarily be those within or linked to the military community or perhaps your local networking group, for example. Some of the best networks for support are found at places you would never expect – that could be your local church or children's school. You might be a keen sportsperson or rock the local pub quiz – whatever your "thing" is, make those connections and nourish them. They might not pop up as 'traditional' business networks but they can prove to be just as valuable. That's because they can help reduce the isolation that typically comes with self-employment, as well as keep you inspired and – potentially make a sale.

THE NETWORKS THAT ARE IMPORTANT TO YOU.

Spend some time listing out any communities you are already a part of that might be able to help you in your business journey.

Next, note down whether they're direct business networks or personal networks. Maybe they are there to help you stay inspired or perhaps to show support. Then, add how you are showing up to help those networks, too. Just remember, you get out what you put in, so get stuck into that community and make the best connections you can.

2020 was a challenging year but we had some real successes along the way, too. And, if that's what we can achieve during a pandemic, just think about what we can get done from now on with a little help from our friends.

24

THE BEST BUSINESS TIPS
FROM PODCAST GUESTS

"If your actions inspire others to dream more, learn more,
do more and become more, you are a leader."
– *John Quincy Adams. Sixth President of the United States*

Is there anything worse than being lectured to by someone who hasn't got any experience in that particular subject? There are so many people out there doing it and it's one of my biggest bugbears – people who go on one course and think they are an expert. Grrr!!!

There's nothing more confusing to a business owner who's been around for a few years, suddenly finding themselves being given business advice from someone who's never even had a business. Seriously, it happens more often than you think!

For me, it's as foreign as setting up a breastfeeding group without ever seeing a baby! You just wouldn't do it without the proper experience and, even then, you'd need a variety of it. And yes, you could read a book or go on a course about it, but can you really help people without any real-life experience?

I am hoping by now you've realised that I have been around the block a bit – in both my entrepreneurial life and, of course, my pesky Armed Forces life. But, like all good 'experts' there's an awful lot I don't know so I'm not going to just guess the parts that I'm not completely sure of. So, that's where I call on my pals to help me out in this book.

I believe that there's nothing like learning from those who have come before you. On the podcast series, I have interviewed over 60 members of our fantastic community, many of whom are running their own amazing businesses. So, before this book comes to an end, I wanted to share with you some of their best business tips – there's nothing better than reading advice from the people who know what they're talking about!

SUZY OLIVIER – FOUNDER OF MOTHERS OF ENTERPRISE

Know Your Why

You have to know your why – I think that's for anything in life. If you're starting a new exercise regime or a new job, or you're thinking about a new business, you have to know your deep-rooted why for doing it.

Dean Graziosi says that you have to ask yourself 'why' seven times in order to get to your deep reason 'why'. So, whatever your answer is, ask again for an answer and keep going deeper and deeper until you get to where you're in the heart feeling of why you're doing it, because business is hard. There really are times when you want to say: "This was too much; I can't do this anymore. It's too hard. It's too difficult, too stressful, too overwhelming," and everything in you will be screaming to just walk away. But when you know in your heart why you're doing something, and that mission is so big and so rooted in you, it keeps you going... especially once you know that you're doing it for the right reasons.

Does your business have appeal?

This is so often overlooked, especially in the micro-business arena where you validate your idea to so many people. If they love it and it excites them, it will most likely excite the world, too. Some people will put a lot of money, time and effort into building something before launch, only to have the tumbleweed rolling on. Then they feel terrible. So, validate it. Do your market research. We're living in a time now where you can access millions of people through Facebook and Twitter even when you're on the go. It's never been easier to reach the people you want to do business with, with the click of a button.

So know your 'why', validate it and then the rest is relatively easy. All the information is out there for building a business; you just need strong foundations before you do anything on top of it.

Does your business fit your lifestyle?

The question I often ask people is: does this business that you're thinking of starting honestly fit your lifestyle? I see spouses here and there start businesses, and then their partner has come home with a surprise posting saying they're leaving in six weeks and they're thinking, 'Oh, but I've only just built my business in this location.' You need to ensure that what you're starting is a viable, sustainable business. Knowing your lifestyle is one thing. Having a fantastic business idea and even validating it, knowing that the market wants it, is key when starting a new business but, if it cannot move around with you, are you able to pack it up and take it to a new location so that you can keep it going? If not, you'll be faced with the fact that you are going to have to start from scratch again. Starting a company from scratch, especially a service-based business, every two years or less will be forever draining.

That's why my advice is to organise the timetable for the year ahead and see what that business looks like, assuming that it is going to be a success. Does it allow for moving? Does it allow you to be home with your kids? Does it allow you to take weekends off? Does it allow you not to have to work every single day for ten hours a day?

So often, we build businesses that we think are a really, really good idea and then a year or two down the line, we realise we're in a job that we're essentially trapped by and it's even worse than a job because you can't get out of it since the whole thing relies on you! That's why it's important to know what you want from your business and make sure that this business fits into your life rather than your life fitting into the business. I've been there, and it's really, really horrible when you think you can't call in sick today, MY business needs ME to show up. So just make sure that it fits your idea of a good, healthy balance with a new lifestyle and not the other way around.

DR GILLIAN JONES – GILLIAN JONES DESIGNS
Presentation is important.

I get a lot of positive feedback on my packaging and the little notes I put in with my products. Obviously, this is for a product business, but the same applies to others.

I always put a little handwritten note in with each purchase to say thank you very much for their order, referencing the order specifically so they know that it's not just a generic note that is sent out to everyone.

I make sure I've got little stickers with my logo on so it all looks neat, branded and like a proper fine art print should since it's a relatively expensive product, so people expect a relatively expensive-looking package to arrive to their door. That's why I try to meet that without spending too much money. That's of number one importance to me.

The way your business presents itself also includes things like emails as well, such as your email signature block, for example. So, be sure to create something that looks professional and neat and, if you've got one, include your logo to start building that brand association.

Communicating with your clients and customers

Communication is key in anything and everything that you do. Letting people know something's going to be delayed or providing them with progress updates is pretty important. There have been numerous occasions in which I've had to contact someone to say: "I'm really sorry. I've been in hospital/ill and I'm not going to get this done in time" and, 99% of the time, people are absolutely fine with that. People are nicer and more understanding than you think they're going to be.

Being completely open about it just breaks down that barrier and people aren't then wondering what's going on or why you may have disappeared off the face of the earth. I have found that, by doing this, I have managed to retain customers who would perhaps have slipped away should I have chosen to not say anything and, instead, try to keep any issues potentially affecting their orders hidden.

NADINE MONKS – FORCES FAMILY FINANCE

Scheduling your time

You have to be quite ruthless with your time and look at how you will invest it and spend it on people or tasks. Remember to prioritise as well.

I do work hard and work a lot of hours too but, ultimately, the love and the passion are there. If there was ever a time – which happened quite a lot in the early years – where the balance was so off that I felt I was working with no financial reward or not spending any time with my family, that's when I had to re-evaluate my situation.

I think it's also important for people to understand that what your plan was at the beginning or what you want it to be, isn't always where you're going to end up. That's why you have to review it and constantly self-evaluate because, nine times out of ten, if there's a problem in the business or if it's not going as you'd hoped it would, a lot of the time, it's probably down to you and what you are doing or not doing. Having that self-realisation is really important.

Nadine used to describe herself as being time short so, as a tool to help her decide what step to take next in business, she used the **SMART** method – **S**pecific, **M**easurable, **A**chievable, **R**ealistic and **T**ime driven.

I think it's something that many of us already do intuitively but, when you're making those decisions, you're very conscious of SMART. So, for example, you might want to buy a house. Well, that's great, but if you're not a little more specific about where you want to live and how much you want to spend, for example, it might make things a lot harder. That's why it would be worth asking yourself these questions: is that actually achievable? Have you done your research? Could you ever afford that? Is that realistically within your grasp, even if hard work is involved?

It's important to also look at the time scale of it all as well. Once you've decided what it is you want to do: is it realistic and can I achieve it? Having a specific time scale makes you accountable to yourself and means that the goal will be realistic and measurable. So, keep constantly checking in with them. Is it SMART?

In all honesty, you can apply the SMART method to anything, even things we do all the time on a daily basis. Take food shopping for a dinner party for example. Let's be realistic... Is it going to take you 20 minutes to achieve? Once you've parked up, queued to get in, all the rest of it? No, it isn't.

So, be realistic with it. Make a list, look at your budget, get in the shop, get what's on that list and get out. That's the way that I approach pretty much every task I do in my life. As dull as that sounds, it just seems to work in the background of my mind, just doing that fabulous thing that most women are good at... multitasking. Just how many birds can I kill with this stone?

JESSICA SANDS – FOUNDER OF MILSPO NETWORK CIC

And then there's little ol' me – here's what I think I would answer if I were asked to share my top business tip in an interview. I must admit, my best tip is stolen from my friend, who I interviewed for the podcast in 2019.

*JKFG – Just Keep F****** Going!*

My wonderful friend, Jody Jones – who was a swimmer, singer and generally brilliant human being – swam the English Channel in 2019 for 18 hours and 14 minutes, all whilst enduring stage 4 bowel cancer and undergoing her 22nd cycle of chemotherapy.

Jody sadly died in November 2022. My heart will always be a little bit broken without Jody here but her ongoing legacy and the fact that she just kept going, despite what life threw at her, is a testament to how epic she was and how much we should listen to her words.

And that's because the Armed Forces and entrepreneurial life is, I imagine, a little bit like swimming the Channel. No, you don't get as wet, but there are pockets of tides that work with you, bringing you closer to that goal but, inevitably, there are the brutal waves we have to battle against and the odd jellyfish sting that we have to bounce back from. **The secret is... just keep f****** going.**

"What sets you apart
can sometimes feel
like a burden,
and it's not.
And a lot of the
time, it's what
makes you great."

– Emma Stone.

Academy and Golden Globe Award-winning actor

PART FOUR

So here we have it, OUR own book! Together, we've managed to create something VERY special. Yes, they may be my words printed on these pages but, with your added ingenuity, they have become ours. It's a place where your dreams have been mapped out, where your ideas have been awoken and scribbled down, and you have an exciting start to your new business journey.

But this is only the start and, as epic as military spouses and partners are, I'm afraid this is the bit where my words end and your hard work begins. But this is not goodbye – you won't be completely alone on your journey. There is a whole community of us here and ready for you, and we are all so excited to see what you are building. We cannot wait to support you and watch you achieve everything you deserve in your business.

You are now officially a Milspo member!

You are an entrepreneurial military spouse, partner or

other-half, and you have joined the best team in the world!*

I can't promise that it'll all be plain sailing from here though. You have read all about the roller coaster journey that me and my pals have had leading up to this point. Military life will test you and entrepreneurial life will more than test you but, quite honestly, it's worth every moment. So, get ready for the most epic experience – that of running your own business. And, with the help, accountability and wonderful community over at Milspo, you're certainly in safe hands.

I am SO proud of your achievements and where the journey will take you next. Don't forget to keep me updated so I can celebrate with you.

And remember…

*'This negative voice in my head isn't my truth. I **can** do this and I **will** do this – **just watch me go!**'*

As you've now told yourself, you can do this and I honestly can't wait to watch where the next chapter takes you!

* Yes, you may think I'm just being biased but it's the truth. You'll see! And I promise I won't say "I told you so" when you start thinking it, too.

248

GLOSSARY

EXPLAINING THOSE MILITARY TERMS

Admin order
A formal document issued to serving personnel containing details of a duty that they've been instructed to attend, such as a course or exercise, which could be anywhere within the UK or overseas.

Decompression
The process of helping serving personnel adapt to their home environment in a gradual way following a deployment, especially if it has been a particularly long time or within a stressful environment. It's also a good opportunity for personnel to be observed and signposted should they need further support as a result of what they have experienced whilst away.

Deployment/Detachment/Tour
This is when serving personnel are tasked to go on operation (a specific, often highly intense, task that is considered to be of high importance to the country it is in) anywhere in the world for any duration of time, from a few weeks to many, many months. Families are not allowed to join their serving family member on deployment.

Med-evac
Short for medical evacuation.

Military quarter
Housing that accommodates eligible serving personnel and their families each time they are sent to live in a new location as a result of the serving person's posting.

Patch
A group of housing consisting of military married quarters. Sometimes located on or next to, a military base, but some can be found well away from operational bases. A legacy from a time of a bigger Armed Forces.

Posting
When serving personnel are sent to their next job, which is often in a different location. Families can choose whether to join their serving member on their posting.

POTL/PODL
Short for post-operation tour/deployment leave. This is additional leave awarded to the service person based on how long they have been deployed for.

Posting notice
A term used for a military assignment order that confirms the serving person's next job.

Royal British Legion
A charity that supports members and veterans of the British Armed Forces, financially, socially and emotionally.

25

BONUS CHAPTER – BRANDING FOR YOUR BUSINESS

"Your brand is what people say about you
when you're not in the room."

– Jeff Bezos. Founder of Amazon

Since I'm a graphic designer, I've decided to add a little bit of my design expertise to this book – I mean, what could be more beneficial to your new business than a little bit of help with your branding?

WHAT IS BRANDING?

Branding is so much more than just your logo. It includes every single touch point that your client encounters with your business. It's how your business makes your clients feel, think and engage with your services and/or products. It's not just about the physical stuff, like beautifully designed packaging and products. It's also about the language you use, the quality of the service you provide/the products you create and the overall experience your clients receive. Branding is a vast subject – worth a book in its own right to be honest and I know there are many out there.

However, as a qualified graphic designer, I am just going to focus on the visual stuff – my area of expertise. And, for the sake of this chapter, when I talk about branding, I am talking about the visual aspect of it – your logo, fonts, colours, styling – all of the design parts of your business.

In this chapter, I will also give you some tips should you choose to DIY your first brand design and I'll also explain the three pillars that form the foundations of your brand design. These are the logo, font and colour.

First up, I need to say that branding is so vital to the success of your business and, I believe, that it should be one of the things that you seriously consider outsourcing to a professional as soon as you are in a position to do so.

> *"If you think good design is expensive,*
> *you should look at the cost of bad design."*
> — *Dr Ralf Speth. A German automotive executive*
> *and director of the Indian company, Tata Sons*

I promise I am not just saying this because my business relies on people outsourcing their branding design but because I have seen first-hand how bad design can ruin a brand and how good design can propel it. Remember when we talked about Victoria Beckham's posh white T-shirt in chapter 5 and how it isn't expensive if the right person wants to buy it? That's got everything to do with branding and how a client sees the company's value.

However, I am also aware that when you start up, cash can be sparse and you may not have the capacity to commission a designer straight away. In that case, you might want to give DIY branding a go before you make some income and head to the professionals. So let me give you the best chance to do that.

DIY'ING YOUR NEW BRAND

By now, you've probably worked your way through the first section of this book. You'll have found your reason for starting a business, you'll have decided on your business's name, bagged your website and social media pages and you may have even started selling your products or services, too. That means it's time to get something visual to represent your business. So, let's start with the basics – the personality of your business.

BRAND STYLING

Before you do anything, you need to think about the 'feel' of your new business and what others will expect it to 'feel' like visually. It's all about the research.

You will have your previous research from the first section of this book. Use that data to start collating images and inspiration about what you would like your branding to look like. Grab your favourite magazines and a pair of scissors, or head to Google and Pinterest so that you can get printing and collate a selection of images, colours, fonts and designs that inspire you and fit with the research you did about your business in Part One.

GETTING TO KNOW YOUR BRAND

Here's the design questionnaire I send out to all my new branding clients before I start working with them – I'm sure you will find it helpful, too. So, grab a cuppa, a pen and your notebook; find your favourite corner of your home and start filling out the questions below with as much honesty and in as much detail as you can.

1. **Tell me about your business!** What is its name, strapline (if you have one that you want to be included in your design)

and what does your business do? Remember, this is not your corporate 'About' page. Instead, this should be along the same lines the lines of your elevator pitch. What would you say if you had just 30 seconds in an elevator to explain your business to a potential client or customer?

2. **What problem do you solve for your customers?**

3. **Is there a unique story behind your business, business name or existing logo?**

4. If you have an existing brand/identity, **why isn't it working for you?**

5. **Share five adjectives or words that best describe your business.**

6. **Do you have specific guidelines** – the do's and don'ts about colour or other elements of brand identity?

7. **Who are your three main competitors (direct or indirect)?** What do you like about their presence? What do you dislike about their brand identity? It is important to see what your competition looks like compared to the industry standard. Your client must recognise your business for the field it is in rather than confusing it for something else because it is 'too original'.

8. **Are there any other ideas or design elements you'd like to add?**

MOOD BOARD

By now, you will have loads of notes about your business and the type of branding you might create. But, before you get stuck into creating your new logo, there's just one more little process I want you to go through – refining your ideas.

It would be so easy to throw everything into one design but the true beauty of quality design is also what's not included. So I want you to collect together all your notes, images and ideas and create your new branding mood board. It can be a digital or physical one but the key here is to examine each piece and ask yourself: *"Does this really fit with my business and its feel?"* You know your business better than anyone so, if it doesn't fit, get rid! It might be beautiful but if it doesn't feel right, it will stick out like a sore thumb in the short term, annoy you in the medium term and, in the long run, put off your dream clients and customers. Believe me, this is something that you will thank me for later.

You should now have a refined, beautiful mood board filled with inspiration that will accompany you throughout this whole process. So, are you ready to start designing?

At this point, I will interject to say that if you are going to commission a professional, now is the time to find them. The process you have done up to this point will be absolutely invaluable to them and together you can work towards a brief that uses all of your research. Don't be tempted to commission anyone without doing this process first. Yes, the designer will also be doing their own research, but there's nothing better than adding that to your own – after all, you know your business best.

I also want to add that, at this point, any professional designer worth their cost will be doing their own research around colour psychology. Now that's a whole other book subject in itself but I would recommend, if you are continuing down the DIY route, to have a look at some of the ideas around colour and branding.

Right then, are you ready? Let's start designing!

FOUNDATION NO. 1 – YOUR LOGO

Your logo is the one element of your branding that you will probably use most often but it's only a cornerstone of your completed brand. It should be entirely unique for your business (please don't take the easy route and download a template – your business deserves so much more than that!) and it should be easily recognised by your clients.

The easiest way to start designing your logo is to grab a pencil and start drawing. Don't get distracted by any online creative software at this point – a pencil and paper are what's best. Make sure your mood board isn't too far away so that you can stay inspired as you sketch.*

The best, most effective logos are simple and distinctive – just think of Nike, Apple and Virgin: clear, easily recognisable and distinct. You don't need to add everything to your logo design as this will just complicate things. Yes, you can add a simplified icon if you like but be sure to keep it simple. Just think about the brands I mentioned above. Have you used the right style of font? Does it feel like your business? Some of the best logos around are simply typographic-based (or words-based). You don't always need to add an icon.

However, now is the time to add your strapline (if you are using one) but, in the absence of one, you will need a second option, called a secondary logo.

Do you have a collection of colours that you might like to use that reflect your business? Of course, you won't want to use all of them in your logo (we'll be discussing brand colours shortly), but a stand-out brand colour will attract your clients more easily once they have that recognition.

By the end of this process, you should have a fair idea on the look of your new logo. Does it honestly feel like your business? You don't need to look at it and know straight away what that business does – that's something that we will build with brand recognition (just look at the Apple logo – they certainly don't sell fruit but they've created a business around the recognition of that icon).

Are you happy with it? There's still time to work on and tweak it, as the next step is converting your ideas and drawings into a digital version. You'll need a digital version so that it can be scaled when you come to designing and creating the marketing for your business. The best way to create your logo is using a design software programme such as Adobe Illustrator. However, there are other digital options you can use to draw your logo. Canva is one (but please avoid using any premade elements), or you can outsource this element to a designer.

They will have a wide range of typography options that you can use for your logo. You can amend your typography choices now and I would recommend picking something different from the traditional system fonts. You can find font foundries online that specialise in designing fonts and it's here that you can purchase a licence to use them. So not only will you have something more bespoke but you can also be assured that you can use it legally to create your logo(s) and for commercial use. You could temporarily use free font sites, such as DaFont, but avoid using them for your final design as they are generally for personal use only. You will need to search out the professional font foundries to buy a licence from them. This is another reason why downloading template logos is a bad idea – you never know where that font has come from.

Now that you have your finalised logo in a digital format, it's time to get practical. You will need to recreate your new logo in black, white and any other brand colours that you think might be relevant.

You will need to use your logo on many things, so you'll need some different file types.

For printing
You will need to download your logo as a vector for printing (usually a .pdf, an .eps or an .svg file). Any of these will be perfect for printing but I recommend you download all the options so that you have access to them in the future. Then, convert all of your text to outlines and export it as each of these files. These are the files you can scale to any size.

For online work
You may not be surprised to hear that .jpgs are your pals here, along with .pngs, which have transparent backgrounds. You will be using these online for your social media content and overall designing. They are created from pixels, so they won't be able to scale up as well as the print files, but they are perfect for online use.

FOUNDATION NO. 2 – YOUR TYPOGRAPHY
Second to your logo, in terms of usage, is your typography options. There are millions of font choices out there but simplicity is key to ensuring your brand looks professional. Again, thousands of fonts might be out there but that doesn't mean we need to use them all!

Here's the list of fonts you will need to pick for your new brand:

Primary font – by now, you will have a logo that probably includes a font of some type. Depending on its styling, you will want to use this for the designs in your brand. That might be as a primary font for titles and highlights or a decorative font to be used sparingly.

Secondary fonts – you should have one or two options for things such as the body copy In your leaflets or on your website. This should be easily legible but still feel like your business.

Accent or decorative font – this one is only to be used on special occasions. Don't go bonkers! It'll add interest and style but it can move into overwhelm if used on too many things. Make sure it's actually legible. There are loads of pretty fonts out there but your clients and customers will still need to be able to read them. Consider letters such as 'a' and 'g'. If you are creating products or services for children, you might want to pick a font option with a simpler 'a' and 'g', rather than 'a' and 'g'.

When picking your fonts, look at all different type settings and how they work in another case – **bold** or *italic*, for example. You might want to choose a traditional serif font (with flicky bits) or something more modern, like a sans serif (sans = without, serif = flicky bits).

You might want to see what they look like with larger leading (the space between each line, from back in the day when a printer used a strip of lead to space the lines on a printing press) or changing the k e r n i n g (the distance between each letter.) Fun fact, it is a word that is believed to come from a French term of a Latin word meaning 'corner' or 'hinge'.

Fonts usually come in different font weights. You can often find simple fonts with beautiful options as an italic and don't underestimate what a font will look like in UPPERCASE, too. With the right kerning, it can look very sophisticated.

Finding your perfect font can be a long process, so make sure you have your mood board close by to help you stay inspired and, most of all, enjoy it! Once you get going, I'm certain you will find a new love for typography.

Top tip: don't forget to check the licences on ALL of your fonts to ensure that you can use them legally within your business.

Keep a record of the names of your new brand fonts. You'll need them every time you design something yourself or outsource any design work.

FOUNDATION NO. 3 – BRAND COLOURS

Colour is crucial to any brand, especially when used creatively and consistently. Just think of any of your favourite brand's colours. The welcoming navy blue of a flight attendant, the excitement of the red flash of a stiletto, the flicker of a purple chocolate wrapper... they add so much to a brand.

You may already have a solid attachment to colour. For example, the Milspo brand colours are based on the suffragette movement's green and purple. The podcast was launched 100 years after women's suffrage, so it seemed a fitting tribute for the project. In Milspo's case, the purple also reflects the tri-service nature of the brand, as well as the original meanings of the colours – purple stood for loyalty and dignity, white for purity and green for hope. Or, perhaps you might follow the research you conducted when reading about colour psychology, working alongside what you have pinned to your mood board. Either way, like your logo, colour simplicity here is key.

You'll want to pick between one and three main colours as well as a few complementary colours to back them up. Think about how you'll use the colours and how they will be applied to your marketing. For example, maybe you want one stand-out accent colour in your logo, which would be perfect for your accent font. Perhaps you need a good base colour for your backgrounds that complements that intense accent colour without competing with it. Look at a colour wheel. Picking opposites on the wheel adds interest and contrast.

Remember that there are no right and wrong colours. It's your brand and you get to pick what you feel is best, but do try to limit them to a few colour options. Use too many and it instantly loses its simplicity and quality.

You will now have a complementary colour palette that reflects your brand and complements your logo and typography style. But, to ensure they are consistent between everything you use, you'll need to note down the unique colour codes.

If you've ever done DIY design in the past, you'll know that guessing your brand colours just doesn't work. You'll end up with multiple options of 'the same' colour that isn't actually the same at all and, before you know it, you've spent hours clicking away trying to make things match. That's really NOT ideal for a busy business owner.

But did you know that designers have special codes that remove the need for guesswork? Codes that you can use on a day-to-day basis for your branding?

You've probably heard of Pantone references and RGB (red, green and blue) breakdowns – but did you know about HEX codes and CMYK? And what on earth do they even mean?!

Pantone – this company is best known for its Pantone Matching System (PMS), which is used across various industries. Basically, it is a universal colour coding system in physical and digital formats that anyone can reference to ensure that the colour matches on any surface – coated and uncoated materials, cotton, polyester, nylon and plastics. You don't need to be an expert in this but you will at some point be asked for them by a supplier, so make a note somewhere that you'll remember.

Web colours are colours used in displaying graphics and imagery on websites and digital platforms. Colours are sometimes specified as an RGB or in a HEX format (#).

RGB – red, green and blue primary light colours are combined in various ways to reproduce a broad array of colours. The primary purpose of RGB colours is to display images in electronic systems, such as televisions and computers, though they have also been used in conventional photography.

HEX codes are similar to RGB codes but use numbers and letters according to the intensity of their red, green and blue components, each of which is represented by eight digits. These are used primarily on websites.

CMYK are the inky ones! That's right. The colour breakdowns for printing that uses cyan (C), magenta (M), yellow (Y) and, of course, black (K?!). Can you guess why we use a 'K' for black? Sadly, it's not because it might get confused with the 'B' in blue. It's actually to do with the 'key' plate and lining things up... another bit of designer knowledge that could come in handy for a pub quiz one day.

Now, this can sometimes get confusing and there are other types of less-used codes but, as long as you note them all down and use them consistently, eventually, over time, they'll start to make more sense when it comes to what does what and what goes where.

BRAND GUIDELINES/BRAND BIBLE/STYLE GUIDE

Now that you have your brand foundations, it's time to collate them all into one place because, I promise you, you will need easy access to them very soon. It's time to grab a notebook, open a Word doc or anything that will allow you to record some very important details, and make sure you note your colour codes and font names down in one place.

To make it easier, you might want to create a guide that explains everything to do with your brand, breaking it all down on separate easy-to-understand pages. That way, you can add the file to all of your different saved logo files.

Keep backups and working files for anything you design. You will need them one day. It's also a good idea to name your logo files in a way that explains what does what. Some design files that you download won't open without the correct design software (.eps files, for example), so you will need to know what is what when you get to the point that you need to design with it.

It all might sound exhausting but, I promise, this will make it all a lot easier in the long run.

But, that's not all. There are other elements you could add to your guide.

ADDITIONAL ELEMENTS OF BRAND

So, I've talked through the three key pillars of your brand – the logo, typography and colour – as well as what to consider if you're a new start-up, and these are the perfect foundations to get you going on your branding. Eventually, you will want to build on these foundations by looking at and sourcing some photography, business-relevant icons, illustrations, patterns and textures. This is a living project that will grow as your business grows, so I am wary of encouraging you to source and pay for these things straight away. Instead, you will want to keep these additional elements in your mind as you market your business. Like the three pillars, you'll want to match the style of any other elements to that of your mood board.

HOW TO MAKE IT LOOK LIKE IT'S BEEN DESIGNED BY A PRO

Whether using DIY'd branding or having it created by a professional, there is most likely still lots of parts of your marketing that you will be doing yourself. Here are some tips that designers tend to use when creating work for businesses so that you can apply them to your own marketing.

A pro sticks to the brand's fonts – no more, no less! There's nothing more amateur than a design that uses a million random fonts. It's a big giveaway that it's not been professionally created and will be confusing and overwhelming for the reader to digest. In the same way that using only one font can be boring, using too many is a right turn-off. Stick to the two or three brand fonts that you initially chose. It'll make a considerable difference to your design.

Designers only use the brand's colours – again, just like with the fonts, it can be overwhelming if there are too many. However, the right use of a single colour can be hugely influential. So be brave and maybe stick to one brand colour.

They keep it simple – too much is never a good thing! A cluttered design with too much text or images dilutes the appeal.

HIRING A PROFESSIONAL DESIGNER

You might feel like you've reached the point where your time would be better spent on other parts of your business and you would like to outsource your designing to a brand or graphic designer. Firstly, let me say that this is amazing news! But, before you pick anyone, be sure to make every effort to choose the right designer.

It's going to take more than a recommendation from your friends... although that's a great place to start! You need to find a designer who works perfectly with you and your business, and can deliver the style you are looking for. Do your research. You might find the cheapest option the most attractive but will this person really be the right choice for you? You might even find someone who does other work that you'd be interested in. They might be a web designer or a VA who does graphics, too – are you sure this person can deliver what you need more than a specialist in this area could? Or, perhaps you should come back to them after you've established your brand.

Every designer has their own style and, by using a little research, you can easily find some that match what you are looking for. They should have an up-to-date online portfolio that you can look through to see if you are happy with their work. You don't have to like it all but you should at least find something you love on their site. Do you like the branding that they've created for themselves?

Check out what sort of qualifications they have. If they say they are qualified, find out how and in what specifically. Many self-taught designers have missed out on a lot of industry education and started a business without experience. Also, investigate their design background, as this isn't a regulated industry.

Should any of them mention the word Canva, run for the hills! Seriously, any decent designer should be designing using industry-standard software – this being Adobe InDesign or Adobe Illustrator. Canva is NOT a professional tool. It can be great for some designers to create branded templates for you to use after finalising your branding but creating branding from scratch on Canva translates as using a premade logo template.

Meet up with them, in real life (if possible) or online, to see how well you'll get on. You'll be working together for a fair amount of time, so this is important. Primarily, the designer should ask you questions about your brand so they can glean as much knowledge from you as they need to create your new branding. In my one-to-one briefing meetings, I often ask a vast amount of questions to really allow me to get under the skin of a brand. They should be doing this, too.

Once you are ready to commission a brand designer, get some quotes together. You will want to confirm with the designer what you will actually be receiving from them at the end. Find out how many revisions you get and what happens if you don't like the designs they produce. Talk them through your research and what you expect from them, and the timeline you would like it for.

Generally, like with all things, you get what you pay for. Of course, you could go to an online marketplace to commission a designer but you need to weigh up how important your branding is to your new business. I would stress that sometimes it's better to hold out until you are established and then invest in the proper branding when you have thoroughly explored your new brand. It can sometimes be a considerable investment and, in year one, there are usually more immediate things that need to be paid for.

However you create your branding, know that it will take your idea to the next level. Just remember one thing though: consistency is key. If there's only one thing you take from this chapter, please let it be this phrase. The strength of any brand is how recognisable it is and you can only achieve this by consistently using the same elements of the brand in everything you do. So don't be tempted to add random colours, fonts, logos or anything else for that matter. It will just dilute your brand and confuse your customers and clients.

So that, dear reader, is the beginning of how you brand your new business. It's far from a complete guide but it should push you to get started and create something more than just a logo. Because, after all, your new business will be an extension of you, and you and your business deserve so much more than just one little logo.

* Fear not, no one will judge you on your drawing ability. This is purely just to get your ideas on paper and start developing your new business logo and, of course, overall brand.

THANKS

Firstly, a huge thank you to my editor, Chloe Petrylak, for her added sparkle and for turning my random words into the beautiful sentences on these pages. We did good, my friend!

Thank you to the original disruptors – Heledd Kendrick, Sarah Walker and Helen Massy, and to my podcast guests who helped shape so much of this book: Caroline Hocking, Chris Keen, Eleanor Tweddell, Georgie Muir, Dr Gillian Jones, Grace Selous Bull, Nadine Monks, Polly Charnley, Dr Rosie Gilderthorp, Sarah Stone and Suzy Olivier.

Thank you to the Milspo crew – Abbie, Alex, Caroline, Emma, Gill, Helen, Nadine and Rachel – for inspiring me on a daily basis and making Milspo the epic community that it is today.

Thank you to the Scholar Close gang, the Military Wives Choirs' girls, the hockey girls and the patch girls – in all of the many military postings I've been on over these years! Jo and Lisa, Kate and Penny (you're a Quizzard, Larry!), Nat and Cathryn – I love that wherever we find ourselves, you're there supporting from afar.

Thank you to the mighty Civil Defence HC for always giving me somewhere that feels like home.

To my larger family – the Tyrrells and the Sandses – Dad, Eddie, Mo and Hugh. My original cheerleaders! Thank you!

Thank you to my other sisters, Soph and Houst, for supporting my crazy endeavours despite being on the other side of the world. Your care packages fuelled so many of these words. Remember – NEVER get in the ambulance!

Mr Stanley, a special thanks goes to you, too, for the messages you sent when I needed them most and the karaoke for when I really didn't!

Ann Lush... you rock! Thanks for being there since the student days, and for the nachos.

Thank you to those who never got to read this book. My gorgeous mums, Julia and Gabrielle – you are both missed more than words could ever say. Thank you, Granny, for raising me and being my very first entrepreneurial inspiration. Thank you to my grandpa for all of the sweets and, of course, to beautiful Jody, who always keeps me going. I hope you're all celebrating together.

And a very special thank you goes to my little furry family, Emma, Odin and Freya – our mad house of chaos – for keeping me company and my lap warm whilst I wrote this book.

The last and biggest thank you goes to my wonderful boys – Elliot and Eoin. You're my favourites. It's always all for you xxx

About the Author – Jessica Sands

Jess Sands is the founder of the Milspo Business Network – an online community that inspires and encourages more than 1,300 UK military spouses, partners and other-halves from across the forces world to build successful businesses that flourish and grow despite the pressures of modern military life.

As well as running her creative design business, Design Jessica, Jess is the host of *The InDependent Spouse* podcast – a weekly series of fun, informative podcasts featuring inspiring guests and content provided by individuals who have a link to the military.

Design Jessica is a top 100 Small Business Saturday company and a winner of a Supporting the Unsung Hero Business Award.

Through her work with Milspo, Jess is an #ialso 2019 Top 100 Female Entrepreneur, a finalist of the 2023 Digital Women Awards and was named in *The Telegraph* NatWest 100 Female Entrepreneurs to Watch in 2022. In addition, Milspo was an Equality of Opportunity award winner at the 2022 Women in Defence Awards.

The Milspo Network CIC has signed the Armed Forces Covenant, pledging its support for the Armed Forces community to receive equality and fair treatment when seeking access to public or private goods and services within the UK. As a result, it was awarded Silver Status by the MOD's Employer Recognition Scheme.

Jess lives just outside of London, in her magnolia married quarter, with her RAF pilot husband, Eoin, son, Elliot and cheeky rescue animals Emma, Freya and Odin. When she's not busy building businesses, you can typically find her getting bashed on a hockey pitch or taking the (often frosty) plunge open water swimming in her local lake.

Come and join the best community for military spouses, partners and other–halves that you'll ever need!

Listen to the podcast *(The InDependent Spouse)*
and join in with our weekly events
and, together, let's build that business you deserve.

Find us on Facebook, Instagram and on our website,
or find like-minded businesses to connect with over in our
Find A Milspo Business Directory (www.findamilspo.co.uk).

www.facebook.com/groups/MILSPO

www.instagram.com/milsponetwork

www.milspo.co.uk

Printed in Great Britain
by Amazon

23767520R00156